All About Great Barrier Reef: A Kid's Guide to the Largest Coral System

Educational Books For Kids, Volume 22

Shah Rukh

Published by Shah Rukh, 2024.

While every precaution has been taken in the preparation of this book, the publisher assumes no responsibility for errors or omissions, or for damages resulting from the use of the information contained herein.

ALL ABOUT GREAT BARRIER REEF: A KID'S GUIDE TO THE LARGEST CORAL SYSTEM

First edition. September 29, 2024.

ISBN: 979-8227194916

Written by Shah Rukh.

Table of Contents

Prologue

Welcome to an incredible underwater adventure! Imagine a place so full of color and life that it looks like it was painted by nature itself. The Great Barrier Reef is one of the most amazing wonders of our planet, and it stretches over 1,400 miles along the coast of Australia. It's the largest coral reef system in the world and home to thousands of fascinating creatures, from tiny, colorful fish to enormous sea turtles and even sharks. But it's not just a place for sea creatures; it's a magical underwater world that has stories, secrets, and lessons for all of us.

In this book, we'll dive deep to explore the Great Barrier Reef and discover its many wonders. We'll learn about how it was formed, the incredible animals that live there, and the important role it plays in our world. Along the way, we'll also find out why it's so important to protect this beautiful place and what we can do to help. Whether you've dreamed of snorkeling above the coral or simply love learning about ocean life, this guide will take you on a journey to a place unlike any other.

So, grab your snorkel, and get ready to learn all about the Great Barrier Reef—the largest coral system on Earth and a true treasure of the ocean!

Chapter 1: Exploring the Colorful World of Coral

Coral reefs are one of the most fascinating and vibrant ecosystems on Earth, and the Great Barrier Reef is the largest of them all, located off the coast of Australia. At its heart, corals are small, simple organisms called polyps, but when they come together in huge colonies, they form intricate and beautiful structures known as coral reefs. Corals belong to a group of animals called Cnidarians, which also include jellyfish and sea anemones. While they might look like colorful rocks or plants, corals are living creatures that play a critical role in the marine environment. Their skeletons, made primarily of calcium carbonate, create the framework for the reefs, providing a habitat for countless other species.

The world of coral is a mesmerizing blend of colors, shapes, and textures. Corals come in many varieties, from hard corals that build reefs to soft corals that sway with the ocean currents. Hard corals, like brain coral, staghorn coral, and elkhorn coral, have sturdy, rock-like structures that protect them from predators and the force of the waves. These corals are the architects of the reef, and they form the very foundation upon which the Great Barrier Reef is built. They grow very slowly, often only a few millimeters per year, but over centuries, they can create massive, intricate formations that stretch for thousands of kilometers. Soft corals, on the other hand, do not build reefs but add to the biodiversity of the ecosystem. They are more flexible and come in vibrant hues, creating a beautiful contrast with their hard coral counterparts.

Corals derive their vibrant colors from a special relationship with tiny algae called zooxanthellae, which live inside their tissues. This partnership is mutually beneficial. The algae use sunlight to produce food through photosynthesis, and the corals benefit from this food source, which allows them to grow and thrive. In return, the algae receive shelter within the coral's tissues, protected from the harsh environment of the open ocean. The symbiotic relationship between coral and algae is what gives coral its wide range of colors, from pinks, purples, blues, and reds to the brilliant greens, yellows, and oranges that dazzle divers and marine biologists alike. Without these algae, corals would be mostly transparent or white, as they themselves are colorless. When corals become stressed, such as when water temperatures rise due to climate change, they may expel the algae, causing the coral to lose its color and appear bleached. This is a sign that the coral is unhealthy, and prolonged bleaching can lead to the death of the coral.

The Great Barrier Reef is home to hundreds of species of coral, each with its unique characteristics. Some coral species form large, boulder-like structures, while others grow in delicate, branching shapes that resemble antlers or fans. Some corals even look like massive underwater mushrooms or cabbages, their flat, circular forms adding to the diversity of the reef's landscape. This diversity in coral shapes and sizes creates numerous habitats for other marine creatures, making the reef one of the most biodiverse ecosystems on the planet. The various crevices, tunnels, and overhangs formed by coral provide perfect hiding places for fish, crustaceans, and other sea creatures, ensuring that life on the reef is always bustling with activity.

Coral reefs, like the Great Barrier Reef, are often referred to as the rainforests of the sea, and it's easy to see why. Just as rainforests are teeming with life, coral reefs are filled with a dazzling array of organisms. The coral structures provide food and shelter for thousands of species, from tiny plankton to large fish, sea turtles, and even sharks. Many of these species are specially adapted to life on the reef. Some fish have evolved bright, colorful patterns that allow them to blend in with the coral, while others have developed special feeding habits that make the most of the reef's resources. Parrotfish, for example, use their beak-like teeth to scrape algae off the surface of the coral, while butterflyfish feed on the coral polyps themselves, using their long snouts to reach into the crevices of the reef. This balance of life is crucial for maintaining the health of the coral ecosystem, as each species plays a role in keeping the reef functioning smoothly.

Corals are also responsible for some of the most spectacular underwater events on the planet, such as mass coral spawning. Once a year, usually after a full moon, corals release millions of eggs and sperm into the water in a synchronized event known as spawning. The timing of this event is crucial and is thought to be triggered by environmental cues such as temperature, moonlight, and tides. The water becomes filled with tiny, floating eggs and sperm, which combine to form new coral larvae that will eventually settle on the reef and grow into new colonies. This natural wonder is not only vital for the continuation of coral species but also attracts other marine life to the area, creating a feeding frenzy for fish and other creatures that take advantage of the abundance of food in the water.

In addition to their ecological significance, coral reefs like the Great Barrier Reef are of immense cultural and economic value. For indigenous communities, the reef is a source of food, medicine, and spiritual significance. Many indigenous groups have traditional knowledge of the reef's ecosystems, passed down through generations, and they play an important role in its conservation. Economically, coral reefs support tourism industries, as millions of people from around the world visit places like the Great Barrier Reef to experience its beauty firsthand. Snorkelers and scuba divers come to marvel at the underwater paradise, witnessing the vivid colors and diverse marine life that thrive in these waters. The economic value of coral reefs extends beyond tourism, as they also provide livelihoods for fishing communities and are a source of compounds used in medicine, particularly in the development of treatments for cancer and other diseases.

However, the colorful world of coral is under threat from a variety of environmental pressures. Rising ocean temperatures due to climate change are one of the most significant threats to coral reefs. When water temperatures rise, corals experience stress, which can lead to coral bleaching. While bleached corals are not immediately dead, if the stress continues for an extended period, they are less able to survive. In addition to climate change, coral reefs are also threatened by pollution, overfishing, and destructive fishing practices, such as the use of dynamite or cyanide to capture fish. These activities can cause physical damage to the delicate coral structures, making it harder for the reef to recover and grow. Ocean acidification, caused by increased levels of carbon dioxide in the atmosphere, also poses a serious risk to coral reefs. As the ocean becomes more acidic, it becomes more difficult for corals to build their calcium carbonate skeletons, slowing the growth of the reef and making it more vulnerable to erosion and damage.

Conservation efforts are underway to protect the colorful world of coral, both at the Great Barrier Reef and at coral reefs around the globe. Marine protected areas, sustainable fishing practices, and coral restoration projects are just a few of the ways that scientists, governments, and local communities are working together to preserve these vital ecosystems. Coral nurseries, where coral fragments are grown and then transplanted onto damaged reefs, offer hope for the future of coral reefs. Research into coral genetics and resilience is also helping scientists understand which corals are more likely to survive in warmer, more acidic oceans, allowing for targeted conservation efforts. These efforts are crucial not only for the survival of coral reefs but for the health of the entire marine ecosystem.

The colorful world of coral is one of nature's most spectacular creations, a living structure that supports an incredible diversity of life. Its beauty is unmatched, with corals forming vibrant underwater landscapes that seem almost otherworldly. However, the delicate balance that sustains coral reefs is easily disrupted, and the threats they face are a reminder of the urgent need for action to protect them. By understanding the vital role that coral reefs play in the ocean's ecosystems and working together to preserve them, we can ensure that future generations will continue to marvel at the wonders of the colorful world of coral.

Chapter 2: Amazing Marine Life in the Great Barrier Reef

The Great Barrier Reef is one of the most extraordinary natural wonders of the world, and its vibrant and diverse marine life plays a central role in making it so remarkable. Stretching over 2,300 kilometers along the coast of Queensland, Australia, the reef is the largest coral reef system on Earth. It is a living, breathing ecosystem that is home to an astonishing variety of species, from the tiniest microorganisms to massive marine mammals. This vast underwater world teems with life, and each species plays a role in maintaining the delicate balance of the reef's ecosystem. The Great Barrier Reef supports more than 1,500 species of fish, 400 species of coral, 4,000 species of mollusks, and thousands of other marine creatures, many of which are found nowhere else on the planet.

Fish are the most visible inhabitants of the Great Barrier Reef, and their diversity is staggering. From tiny, brightly colored fish that dart among the corals to larger predatory species that patrol the open waters, the reef is a paradise for fish enthusiasts and marine biologists alike. Some of the most iconic fish species found on the reef include the clownfish, known for its bright orange and white stripes and its symbiotic relationship with sea anemones. Clownfish live among the stinging tentacles of the anemones, where they are protected from predators, while the anemones benefit from the clownfish's waste products, which provide nutrients. Another well-known species is the parrotfish, which gets its name from its beak-like mouth. Parrotfish play a crucial role in maintaining the health of the reef by feeding on algae that grow on the coral. As they scrape away the algae, they prevent it from smothering the coral, helping to keep the ecosystem in balance. The parrotfish also contribute to the formation of sand, as they grind up coral and excrete it in the form of fine sand.

Other fish species are equally fascinating. The butterflyfish, with its vibrant colors and delicate patterns, flits around the coral formations, often feeding on small invertebrates and coral polyps. The angelfish, another strikingly colorful species, is known for its flat, disk-shaped body and the wide variety of patterns and hues it displays. There are also the larger, more intimidating species, such as the barracuda, a fast and powerful predator with sharp teeth and a sleek, streamlined body that allows it to hunt with incredible speed. Barracudas are often seen patrolling the waters around the reef, waiting for an opportunity to strike at smaller fish. Then there is the giant grouper, one of the largest species of bony fish found in the world. Weighing up to several hundred kilograms, these massive fish are slow-moving but powerful hunters that feed on other fish, crustaceans, and even small sharks.

Beyond the dazzling array of fish, the Great Barrier Reef is home to numerous species of sharks and rays, both of which play important roles as apex predators. Sharks, often misunderstood as dangerous to humans, are essential for maintaining the health of the reef by keeping fish populations in check and preventing any one species from becoming too dominant. The most commonly seen species include the reef shark, which is relatively small and often spotted by divers, and the larger tiger shark, which is known for its distinctive stripes and its wide-ranging diet that includes fish, birds, and even sea turtles. Another fascinating shark species found in the Great Barrier Reef is the wobbegong, or carpet shark, which has a flat, camouflaged body that allows it to blend in with the ocean floor. Wobbegongs are ambush predators, lying in wait for prey to swim by before striking. Rays, including the graceful manta ray, are another highlight of the reef. With wingspans that can reach up to seven meters, manta rays glide effortlessly through the water, feeding on plankton and small fish. They are often seen performing acrobatic flips and rolls, a spectacle that leaves divers in awe of their beauty and agility.

In addition to fish, the Great Barrier Reef supports a wide variety of marine mammals. Dolphins are common around the reef, and they can often be seen swimming in pods, using their echolocation abilities to hunt for fish and squid. Their playful nature and intelligence make them a favorite among visitors to the reef. The dugong, a close relative of the manatee, is another marine mammal found in the Great Barrier Reef. Dugongs are herbivorous creatures that feed on seagrass, and their gentle, slow-moving nature has earned them the nickname "sea cows." Despite their peaceful existence, dugongs are considered vulnerable due to habitat loss and other human-related activities. Protecting their seagrass habitats is crucial for their survival, as well as for the overall health of the reef ecosystem.

Turtles are another beloved species that call the Great Barrier Reef home. Six of the world's seven species of marine turtles can be found in the reef's waters, including the green turtle, the hawksbill turtle, and the loggerhead turtle. These ancient reptiles have been around for over 100 million years, and they play a vital role in maintaining the balance of the marine environment. Green turtles are herbivores, feeding primarily on seagrass and algae, while hawksbill turtles use their sharp beaks to feed on sponges, anemones, and other invertebrates. Loggerhead turtles, on the other hand, are carnivorous, feeding on jellyfish, mollusks, and crustaceans. Marine turtles are known for their long migrations, traveling thousands of kilometers between their feeding grounds and nesting sites. During the nesting season, female turtles come ashore to lay their eggs in sandy beaches, and the sight of hatchlings making their way to the ocean is one of the most heartwarming spectacles of nature.

The invertebrate life on the Great Barrier Reef is just as fascinating as its vertebrate inhabitants. Crustaceans such as crabs, lobsters, and shrimp can be found scuttling along the reef's crevices, using their hard shells to protect themselves from predators. The mantis shrimp, in particular, is a remarkable creature known for its incredible speed and power. Mantis shrimp have specialized limbs that can strike with the force of a bullet, making them formidable hunters despite their small size. These tiny predators are capable of breaking open the shells of mollusks and crabs, and their eyes are among the most complex in the animal kingdom, allowing them to see a wide range of colors, including ultraviolet light.

Octopuses and cuttlefish are among the most intelligent invertebrates found in the Great Barrier Reef. These cephalopods are known for their remarkable ability to change color and texture to blend in with their surroundings, a skill that helps them avoid predators and ambush prey. The reef's cuttlefish are particularly famous for their hypnotic displays, using rapidly changing patterns of light and color to communicate and attract mates. The octopus, on the other hand, is a master of camouflage and problem-solving. With their soft bodies, octopuses can squeeze into the tiniest of crevices to escape danger or hunt for food, and they have been observed using tools and solving complex puzzles in the wild.

Jellyfish, too, play a role in the ecosystem of the Great Barrier Reef. While some species, such as the box jellyfish, are highly venomous and pose a threat to humans, jellyfish are an important food source for many marine animals, including turtles and certain species of fish. The moon jellyfish, a translucent and gentle species, can often be seen drifting through the water, feeding on plankton with its long, trailing tentacles.

The reef's mollusk population is equally impressive, with species ranging from tiny snails to the giant clam, which can grow to over a meter in length and live for more than 100 years. Giant clams are filter feeders, drawing in water through their siphons and extracting plankton and nutrients. Their colorful mantles, which contain symbiotic algae, make them one of the most striking creatures on the reef. The cone snail, on the other hand, is a small but highly venomous predator that uses a harpoon-like tooth to inject venom into its prey.

Despite their dangerous nature, cone snails are also of interest to scientists, as their venom contains compounds that are being studied for use in pain relief and other medical applications.

The Great Barrier Reef's coral species are, of course, the backbone of the entire ecosystem. Corals are living animals that form colonies of polyps, which secrete calcium carbonate to build the reef's structure. The vibrant colors of the coral come from the symbiotic relationship they share with tiny algae called zooxanthellae, which live inside the coral's tissues and provide it with food through photosynthesis. The diverse shapes and forms of the coral provide habitats for countless other species, from small fish to invertebrates. Coral reefs act as nurseries for many marine species, offering shelter and food for juvenile fish and other organisms before they venture out into the open ocean.

Sponges, another type of invertebrate, are also common on the reef. These simple organisms filter water to extract nutrients, playing an important role in maintaining water quality in the reef. Sponges provide habitats for many small creatures and serve as a food source for certain species of fish and turtles.

Sea cucumbers, sea stars, and brittle stars are among the echinoderms that inhabit the Great Barrier Reef. Sea cucumbers are slow-moving creatures that help recycle nutrients by breaking down detritus and organic matter on the seafloor. Sea stars, also known as starfish, are iconic inhabitants of the reef, and some species, like the crown-of-thorns sea star, are known for their role in controlling coral populations. While the crown-of-thorns sea star can sometimes become overabundant and cause damage to coral reefs by feeding on coral polyps, they are also a natural part of the ecosystem when kept in balance.

The Great Barrier Reef is also home to a wide variety of seabirds and marine reptiles, including the sea snakes that glide through the waters, hunting for fish and eels. Many species of seabirds, such as terns and gulls, rely on the reef's fish populations to feed, while others, like the white-bellied sea eagle, are apex predators that hunt fish from above.

In conclusion, the Great Barrier Reef's marine life is a kaleidoscope of diversity and wonder, offering an unparalleled glimpse into the complexity and beauty of the ocean's ecosystems. Each species, from the smallest plankton to the largest sharks, plays an essential role in maintaining the health and balance of the reef, making it a truly extraordinary place on our planet. However, the reef is under threat from climate change, pollution, and human activities, and protecting this incredible ecosystem is vital for preserving its marine life for future generations to marvel at and appreciate.

Chapter 3: How the Reef Was Formed Over Millions of Years

The formation of the Great Barrier Reef, one of the most spectacular natural wonders of the world, is a story that stretches back millions of years. This vast coral system, which extends more than 2,300 kilometers along Australia's northeastern coast, is not only the largest coral reef system on the planet but also a living testament to the power of natural processes that have shaped it over eons. Its formation is the result of a combination of geological, biological, and climatic factors, each playing a role in the reef's development over an extraordinary timescale. Understanding how the reef was formed requires a journey into the distant past, to a time when the planet's climate and geography were vastly different from what they are today.

The Great Barrier Reef, as we see it today, began to take shape about 20,000 years ago, but the foundations for its formation were laid millions of years earlier. The area where the reef now exists was not always underwater. It was, at different points in Earth's history, a terrestrial landscape dominated by mountain ranges and river valleys. Geological evidence shows that the land under the reef was once part of a much older landmass that was exposed above sea level. However, as Earth's climate went through cycles of warming and cooling, sea levels fluctuated dramatically over time, and this played a key role in the formation of the reef.

To understand how the reef was formed, it's essential to explore the dynamic nature of Earth's climate, particularly the ice ages. During periods of glaciation, when large portions of the planet's water were locked in massive ice sheets, sea levels were significantly lower than they are today. In fact, during the last Ice Age, which occurred around 20,000 years ago, sea levels were about 120 meters lower than they are now. At that time, much of what is now the seabed of the Great

Barrier Reef was dry land. Rivers flowed through the landscape, carving valleys and plains that would later become the foundation for the reef's development.

As the climate began to warm and the glaciers melted, sea levels gradually rose. This process, which took thousands of years, submerged vast areas of the continental shelf, including the land that would eventually become the site of the Great Barrier Reef. As the waters rose, they covered the ancient river valleys and floodplains, creating the shallow marine environment that is essential for coral growth. Coral reefs are only able to form in warm, shallow, and clear waters, where sunlight can penetrate and provide the energy necessary for the symbiotic algae that live within coral polyps to thrive.

The process of reef formation begins with tiny marine organisms called coral polyps. These small, soft-bodied creatures belong to a group of animals known as cnidarians, which also include jellyfish and sea anemones. Coral polyps are the building blocks of coral reefs, and they live in large colonies, secreting calcium carbonate (limestone) to create hard, protective skeletons around themselves. Over time, these skeletons accumulate and form the physical structure of the reef. When coral polyps die, their skeletons remain, and new polyps settle on top of them, continuing the process of reef-building. This process of accretion, or the gradual buildup of layers, is incredibly slow, with coral reefs growing at a rate of just a few millimeters to several centimeters per year. Despite this slow growth, over millions of years, the accumulation of coral skeletons can result in the formation of massive reef structures.

The initial stages of the Great Barrier Reef's formation likely began when coral polyps settled on the submerged remnants of ancient mountains and river valleys. These underwater features provided a solid substrate for the corals to attach to, allowing them to establish colonies. As the corals grew and expanded, they formed fringing reefs, which are reefs that grow directly along the coastline. These early reefs were likely much smaller than the vast structure we see today, but they laid the groundwork for future growth.

One of the most important factors in the formation of the Great Barrier Reef was the slow but steady rise in sea level following the end of the last Ice Age. As the glaciers continued to melt and sea levels rose, the coral colonies were able to grow upwards and outwards, following the rising waters. This process of vertical growth is crucial for coral reefs, as they can only survive in shallow waters where sunlight is abundant. If sea levels rise too quickly, coral reefs can be drowned, as they are unable to grow fast enough to keep pace with the rising water. However, during the post-Ice Age period, sea level rise was gradual enough to allow the corals to thrive and continue their upward growth.

The process of coral reef formation is also influenced by biological factors, particularly the symbiotic relationship between coral polyps and microscopic algae called zooxanthellae. These algae live within the tissues of the coral polyps and provide them with nutrients through photosynthesis, a process that requires sunlight. In return, the coral provides the algae with a protected environment and access to the waste products they need for photosynthesis. This symbiotic relationship is what allows coral reefs to flourish in nutrient-poor waters, as the algae are able to convert sunlight into energy that sustains the coral. Without this relationship, the Great Barrier Reef would not have been able to form in its current location, as the surrounding waters are relatively low in nutrients.

The formation of the Great Barrier Reef is also closely tied to the region's climatic conditions. Coral reefs thrive in warm, tropical waters, and the Great Barrier Reef benefits from the consistently warm sea temperatures in the Coral Sea. The reef is located in an area that is sheltered from the cold currents that flow from the south, allowing the waters to remain warm enough to support coral growth. Additionally, the clear waters of the region are essential for coral health, as they allow sunlight to penetrate to the depths where the corals live. Sediment and pollution can block sunlight and smother coral reefs, which is why the pristine water quality of the Great Barrier Reef is so important for its survival.

Over time, the process of reef-building continued, with the coral colonies expanding and creating complex structures. The Great Barrier Reef is not a single continuous reef but rather a vast system of nearly 3,000 individual reefs and 900 islands. These reefs vary in size and shape, with some forming massive barrier reefs that extend for kilometers, while others are smaller patch reefs or fringing reefs that grow along the edges of islands. The diversity of reef structures within the Great Barrier Reef is a result of the complex interactions between coral growth, sea level changes, and the underlying geological features of the region.

As the reef grew, it also became home to a wide variety of marine life. The physical structure of the coral provides shelter and habitat for countless species, from tiny invertebrates to large fish and marine mammals. The reef's biodiversity is one of its most remarkable features, and it is estimated that more than 9,000 species call the Great Barrier Reef home. This includes not only the coral polyps themselves but also the fish, mollusks, crustaceans, and other organisms that live in and around the reef. The complex interplay between these species is what makes the reef such a vibrant and dynamic ecosystem.

In addition to biological and climatic factors, the formation of the Great Barrier Reef was also influenced by tectonic activity. The eastern coast of Australia lies along the Indo-Australian tectonic plate, and the movement of this plate over millions of years has contributed to the uplift and subsidence of the land. These tectonic processes have created the underwater topography that the reef now rests upon, including the deep channels, ridges, and submerged mountains that provide the foundation for coral growth. The gradual sinking of the land, combined with the rising sea levels, created the perfect conditions for the reef to expand and thrive.

One of the key stages in the reef's development occurred around 6,000 to 8,000 years ago, when sea levels stabilized at their current level. This period marked the beginning of the modern Great Barrier Reef, as coral growth accelerated and the reef began to take on the form that we recognize today. As the corals continued to grow and accumulate, they created a massive structure that stretches for thousands of kilometers and covers an area of approximately 344,400 square kilometers. The sheer size of the reef is awe-inspiring, and it is often compared to other natural wonders, such as the Amazon Rainforest, in terms of its ecological importance and diversity.

Despite its incredible resilience, the Great Barrier Reef remains a fragile ecosystem that is vulnerable to environmental changes. Climate change, in particular, poses a significant threat to the reef, as rising sea temperatures can lead to coral bleaching, a process in which the coral expels the zooxanthellae algae that it relies on for nutrients. Without the algae, the coral loses its color and can eventually die if conditions do not improve. Other threats to the reef include ocean acidification, which weakens the coral's calcium carbonate skeletons, and pollution from agricultural runoff and coastal development. The future of the Great Barrier Reef depends on our ability to protect and preserve this delicate ecosystem from these and other threats.

In conclusion, the formation of the Great Barrier Reef is a story of natural processes that have unfolded over millions of years. From the ancient landscapes that once stood above the sea to the rise of coral polyps that built the massive reef structures, the reef's formation is a testament to the power of Earth's geological and biological forces. Today, the Great Barrier Reef stands as one of the most diverse and vibrant ecosystems on the planet, but it is also a reminder of the fragility of nature and the need for careful stewardship to ensure its survival for future generations.

Chapter 4: The Importance of Coral Reefs for Ocean Life

Coral reefs are often referred to as the "rainforests of the sea," and for good reason. These extraordinary ecosystems, despite covering less than 1% of the ocean floor, are among the most diverse and productive on the planet. Coral reefs, such as the Great Barrier Reef, play a pivotal role in maintaining the health and balance of the ocean's ecosystems. Their importance extends far beyond their immediate boundaries, as they provide habitat, food, and protection for a vast array of marine life, influence global fish populations, and even contribute to human economies. Coral reefs are a keystone of ocean life, and understanding their significance helps illuminate the intricate connections that sustain marine environments. The continued existence of coral reefs is vital not only for the ocean's biodiversity but also for the overall health of the planet.

At the heart of coral reefs' importance is their role as essential habitats for marine life. Coral reefs are home to thousands of species, from tiny invertebrates to large predatory fish. More than 25% of all marine species depend on coral reefs at some point in their life cycle, despite the fact that coral reefs occupy such a small fraction of the ocean's surface. The physical structure of coral reefs, built by the accumulation of calcium carbonate skeletons from coral polyps over thousands of years, creates a complex and three-dimensional environment that offers shelter and protection. The crevices, tunnels, and caves formed by the coral provide hiding places for fish and invertebrates, protecting them from predators and harsh ocean currents. This makes coral reefs a critical nursery for juvenile fish, which find refuge within the coral structures as they grow and mature.

In addition to providing shelter, coral reefs also serve as an abundant source of food for many marine species. Coral polyps themselves are a source of sustenance for some reef-dwelling organisms, but the reef ecosystem is far more complex than that. The reef's intricate food web begins with primary producers like the algae, seagrass, and plankton that grow in and around the coral. These primary producers are consumed by herbivores, such as parrotfish and surgeonfish, which graze on the algae that grow on the reef. In turn, these herbivores are preyed upon by carnivorous species like snapper, grouper, and reef sharks. This chain of consumption creates a balanced and interdependent ecosystem, where each species plays a role in supporting the others.

Coral reefs also act as a vital breeding ground for many species of fish, providing them with the ideal environment for spawning. Reef fish, such as clownfish, butterflyfish, and damselfish, rely on the coral's structure for laying eggs and protecting their young. The larvae of many species begin their lives in the safety of the reef before venturing into the open ocean. The presence of coral reefs, therefore, directly impacts fish populations not only on the reef itself but also in surrounding areas. Many commercially important fish species, including snapper, grouper, and tuna, spend part of their lives on coral reefs. The health of these reefs is directly linked to the availability of fish stocks that support the livelihoods of millions of people around the world, especially in coastal communities that depend on fishing for food and income.

One of the most remarkable aspects of coral reefs is their role in maintaining biodiversity. Coral reefs are home to an extraordinary variety of life, ranging from colorful fish and vibrant corals to less visible but equally important creatures like sponges, mollusks, and crustaceans. In fact, coral reefs are thought to support more species per unit area than any other marine environment, and they are considered one of the most biologically diverse ecosystems on Earth. The biodiversity of coral reefs is crucial because it contributes to the resilience of the ecosystem. Diverse ecosystems are better able to recover from disturbances, such as storms or changes in temperature, because different species can adapt in different ways. This biodiversity also makes coral reefs an invaluable resource for scientific research, as they offer a wealth of information about the interrelationships between species, their adaptations to different environments, and the overall functioning of marine ecosystems.

Beyond their immediate ecological importance, coral reefs play a significant role in maintaining the balance of the entire ocean. Coral reefs are a critical component of the marine food chain, acting as a foundation for the larger marine ecosystem. They support plankton populations, which are the base of the food web and are consumed by a wide range of species, including small fish, which in turn are eaten by larger predators. The health of coral reefs, therefore, has a direct impact on the broader health of ocean ecosystems. Without coral reefs, many species that depend on them for food and shelter would struggle to survive, leading to cascading effects throughout the ocean's food web.

In addition to their role in supporting marine life, coral reefs also act as natural barriers that protect coastal areas from the impacts of waves, storms, and erosion. The structure of coral reefs absorbs the energy of incoming waves, reducing their force before they reach the shore. This protective function is particularly important in tropical and subtropical regions, where many small island nations and coastal communities are vulnerable to storm surges, cyclones, and tsunamis. By buffering coastlines, coral reefs help to prevent flooding, property damage, and the loss of life during extreme weather events. Without coral reefs, many coastal areas would be far more exposed to the destructive power of the ocean, making them more susceptible to the impacts of climate change, such as rising sea levels and increased storm intensity.

Coral reefs also play a role in the global carbon cycle. The calcium carbonate skeletons of coral polyps are formed through a process known as calcification, which involves the absorption of carbon dioxide (CO2) from seawater. This process helps regulate the amount of CO2 in the ocean, which in turn influences the concentration of CO2 in the atmosphere. Coral reefs, therefore, contribute to the moderation of global climate by acting as a carbon sink. However, this process is sensitive to changes in ocean chemistry, particularly ocean acidification, which is caused by the absorption of excess CO2 from the atmosphere. As the ocean becomes more acidic, it becomes more difficult for corals to build their skeletons, threatening the long-term health of coral reefs and their ability to sequester carbon.

The importance of coral reefs extends beyond their ecological role, as they are also vital to human economies, particularly in regions where tourism and fishing are major industries. Coral reefs attract millions of tourists each year, drawn by the opportunity to explore the vibrant underwater world through snorkeling, scuba diving, and glass-bottom boat tours. The revenue generated by reef-based tourism supports local economies, creating jobs and providing income for communities. Additionally, coral reefs contribute to the global fishing industry by supporting fish populations that are harvested for food. Many coastal communities, particularly in developing countries, rely on the fish caught from coral reefs as a primary source of protein. The loss of coral reefs would have devastating economic consequences, particularly for these vulnerable communities.

In addition to their economic value, coral reefs hold cultural and spiritual significance for many indigenous and coastal communities around the world. For example, in the Pacific Islands, coral reefs are considered sacred, and the relationship between people and the reef is deeply rooted in traditional knowledge, practices, and beliefs. Coral reefs are often viewed as living entities that must be respected and protected, and this cultural connection reinforces the need for sustainable management of reef ecosystems. The loss of coral reefs would not only disrupt the livelihoods of these communities but also erode their cultural heritage.

Despite their immense value, coral reefs are under threat from a variety of human activities, including overfishing, pollution, coastal development, and, most significantly, climate change. Rising ocean temperatures are causing widespread coral bleaching, a phenomenon in which corals expel the symbiotic algae that live within their tissues. Without these algae, corals lose their vibrant colors and, more importantly, their primary source of nutrients. If bleaching events are prolonged, the corals can die, leading to the collapse of the entire reef ecosystem. Ocean acidification, another consequence of climate change, is also making it harder for corals to build their skeletons, further threatening the future of coral reefs.

The destruction of coral reefs would have far-reaching consequences, not only for the marine species that depend on them but also for the global environment and human populations. The loss of coral reefs would result in a decline in marine biodiversity, disrupt the food chain, and reduce fish populations, which would have significant implications for food security. Coastal communities would become more vulnerable to storms and flooding, and the economic losses from tourism and fishing would be immense. Furthermore, the disappearance of coral reefs would exacerbate the impacts of climate change by reducing the ocean's ability to sequester carbon.

Conserving and protecting coral reefs is, therefore, a global priority. Efforts to protect coral reefs include the establishment of marine protected areas (MPAs), where fishing and other harmful activities are restricted, and the implementation of sustainable fishing practices that prevent overfishing and the destruction of reef habitats. Additionally, reducing carbon emissions and mitigating the effects of climate change are essential for the long-term survival of coral reefs. Initiatives to restore damaged reefs, such as coral farming and artificial reef structures, are also being developed to help reefs recover from bleaching and other forms of degradation.

In conclusion, coral reefs are indispensable to the health of the ocean and the well-being of human populations. Their role as habitats for marine life, protectors of coastlines, and regulators of the global carbon cycle make them essential to the functioning of the planet's ecosystems. The biodiversity they support, the economic benefits they provide, and the cultural significance they hold all underscore the importance of preserving coral reefs for future generations. However, coral reefs are facing unprecedented challenges, and their survival depends on concerted global efforts to protect and restore these fragile ecosystems. The importance of coral reefs cannot be overstated, and their conservation is critical for maintaining the health and balance of the world's oceans.

Chapter 5: The Threat of Climate Change to the Reef

The Great Barrier Reef, one of the world's most iconic natural wonders and the largest coral reef system on the planet, faces an unprecedented and escalating threat from climate change. This vibrant ecosystem, which stretches over 2,300 kilometers along the northeastern coast of Australia, has long been admired for its stunning diversity of marine life, dazzling coral formations, and ecological significance. However, in recent decades, the Great Barrier Reef has increasingly become a stark symbol of the fragility of coral reefs in the face of global warming. The threat of climate change to the Great Barrier Reef is multifaceted, encompassing rising ocean temperatures, ocean acidification, sea-level rise, and more frequent and severe weather events. These environmental changes are wreaking havoc on the reef's delicate ecosystems, leading to widespread coral bleaching, degradation of marine habitats, and a significant decline in biodiversity. Understanding the full scope of these threats and their impacts is essential to grasping the gravity of the situation facing this unique ecosystem.

One of the most visible and immediate impacts of climate change on the Great Barrier Reef is the phenomenon of coral bleaching, which has become increasingly frequent and severe over the past few decades. Coral bleaching occurs when corals, stressed by higher-than-normal sea temperatures, expel the symbiotic algae known as zooxanthellae that live within their tissues. These algae not only give corals their vibrant colors but also provide them with essential nutrients through photosynthesis. Without the zooxanthellae, corals turn white, hence the term "bleaching." More critically, they lose their primary source of sustenance, which can lead to starvation and, eventually, death if the stressful conditions persist. The frequency and severity of coral bleaching events have been exacerbated by climate change, as global warming has caused ocean temperatures to rise, especially during marine heatwaves.

Since the late 1990s, the Great Barrier Reef has experienced several mass bleaching events, with the most devastating occurring in 1998, 2002, 2016, 2017, and 2020. Each of these events has caused widespread damage to the reef, with large swaths of coral either dying or experiencing severe stress. The 2016 and 2017 bleaching events were particularly catastrophic, with estimates suggesting that over half of the shallow-water corals in some regions of the reef were lost. The northern section of the Great Barrier Reef, which had previously been one of the most pristine and least impacted areas, suffered significant coral mortality during these events. While some corals can recover from bleaching if ocean temperatures return to normal relatively quickly, repeated and severe bleaching events reduce the resilience of the reef, making it harder for corals to bounce back. The cumulative effect of multiple bleaching events over a short period has resulted in a dramatic reduction in coral cover and diversity across large portions of the reef.

The primary driver of coral bleaching is the rise in sea surface temperatures, which has been directly linked to climate change. As the planet warms due to the increasing concentration of greenhouse gases in the atmosphere, the oceans absorb a significant portion of this excess heat. In fact, the ocean has absorbed more than 90% of the heat generated by human-caused global warming since the mid-20th century. Even small increases in water temperature can have profound effects on coral reefs, as corals are highly sensitive to temperature fluctuations. When water temperatures exceed the normal range for an extended period, typically by just 1 to 2 degrees Celsius above the average summer maximum, corals begin to bleach. The Great Barrier Reef is particularly vulnerable to heat stress due to its geographic location in tropical waters, where temperatures are already warm for much of the year. As global temperatures continue to rise, the frequency and intensity of marine heatwaves are expected to increase, putting even greater pressure on the reef's ecosystems.

In addition to rising temperatures, climate change is also driving ocean acidification, another significant threat to the Great Barrier Reef. Ocean acidification occurs as the oceans absorb increasing amounts of carbon dioxide (CO_2) from the atmosphere. When CO_2 dissolves in seawater, it forms carbonic acid, which lowers the pH of the water, making it more acidic. This shift in ocean chemistry has profound implications for coral reefs, as it interferes with the ability of corals to build and maintain their calcium carbonate skeletons, a process known as calcification. Corals rely on the availability of carbonate ions in seawater to form their hard skeletons, but as the ocean becomes more acidic, the concentration of these ions decreases, making it more difficult for corals to grow and repair themselves. Ocean acidification effectively weakens coral structures, leaving them more vulnerable to physical damage from storms, predators, and human activities.

The effects of ocean acidification on the Great Barrier Reef are already being observed, with some studies indicating that calcification rates have declined significantly in recent decades. This reduction in calcification not only affects the ability of corals to thrive but also impacts the overall structural integrity of the reef. A weaker reef structure provides less shelter and habitat for the myriad of marine species that depend on it for survival. Additionally, ocean acidification affects other calcifying organisms within the reef ecosystem, such as mollusks, sea urchins, and certain species of plankton, which are crucial components of the reef's food web. As these organisms struggle to maintain their shells and skeletons in more acidic waters, the entire ecosystem becomes less resilient to environmental stressors.

Another major consequence of climate change for the Great Barrier Reef is the increasing frequency and intensity of extreme weather events, particularly tropical cyclones. Cyclones are a natural part of the weather patterns in the region, but climate change is making these storms more powerful and destructive. Warmer ocean temperatures provide more energy for cyclones, leading to stronger winds, heavier rainfall, and larger storm surges. When a cyclone passes over the reef, it can cause extensive physical damage to coral structures, breaking apart large colonies, dislodging coral fragments, and burying sections of the reef under sand and debris. While coral reefs have evolved to withstand occasional storms, the increasing severity of cyclones due to climate change means that the reef has less time to recover between events. This repeated damage can lead to long-term degradation of the reef's physical structure and biodiversity.

In addition to direct physical damage from storms, climate change is also contributing to rising sea levels, which pose a long-term threat to coral reefs, including the Great Barrier Reef. As global temperatures rise, the polar ice caps and glaciers are melting, and the thermal expansion of seawater is causing sea levels to rise. While coral reefs are generally able to adapt to gradual changes in sea level by growing upwards, the current rate of sea-level rise may outpace the ability of some reefs to keep up. If sea levels rise too quickly, it could lead to a reduction in the amount of sunlight reaching the reef, as corals rely on sunlight for photosynthesis through their symbiotic relationship with zooxanthellae. Without sufficient light, coral growth slows, and the health of the reef deteriorates.

The combined effects of rising temperatures, ocean acidification, extreme weather events, and sea-level rise are placing immense stress on the Great Barrier Reef and its ecosystems. The loss of coral cover and biodiversity has cascading effects throughout the reef's food web. Fish populations that depend on healthy coral habitats for shelter and breeding grounds are declining, which in turn affects the larger predators that rely on these fish for food. The decline in fish populations also has significant implications for the local and global fishing industries, as many commercially important species, such as snapper and grouper, depend on coral reefs at some stage in their life cycle.

The threat of climate change to the Great Barrier Reef extends beyond the environmental impacts; it also poses serious economic and social challenges. The Great Barrier Reef is a vital part of Australia's economy, generating billions of dollars in revenue each year through tourism, fishing, and related industries. Tourism alone supports tens of thousands of jobs in the region, as millions of visitors from around the world come to experience the beauty of the reef through activities such as snorkeling, scuba diving, and boat tours. The decline of the reef due to climate change threatens to undermine this economic lifeline, as damaged and bleached reefs are far less attractive to tourists. Additionally, local communities, particularly those that rely on fishing for their livelihoods, are facing increased uncertainty as fish stocks decline and the health of the reef deteriorates.

The cultural significance of the Great Barrier Reef should not be overlooked either. For Indigenous Australians, particularly the Aboriginal and Torres Strait Islander peoples who have lived in the region for thousands of years, the reef holds deep cultural and spiritual meaning. The health of the reef is intertwined with their traditional practices, stories, and connection to the land and sea. The loss of the reef would not only be an environmental tragedy but also a cultural one, as it would erode the heritage and identity of these communities.

Despite the overwhelming challenges posed by climate change, there are efforts underway to protect and preserve the Great Barrier Reef. Conservation initiatives, such as the establishment of marine protected areas (MPAs) and sustainable fishing practices, are helping to reduce local pressures on the reef. Additionally, scientists are exploring innovative solutions to enhance the resilience of corals to climate change. For example, researchers are investigating the potential for coral breeding programs that select for heat-tolerant coral species, as well as techniques to assist coral recovery after bleaching events.

However, these local efforts alone are not enough to safeguard the reef in the long term. The most effective way to protect the Great Barrier Reef from the impacts of climate change is to address the root cause: the emission of greenhouse gases. Reducing global carbon emissions is essential to slowing the pace of climate change and giving coral reefs a chance to adapt. International agreements, such as the Paris Agreement, which aims to limit global warming to well below 2 degrees Celsius, are critical steps in this direction. However, more ambitious and immediate action is needed to prevent the most severe consequences of climate change for coral reefs.

In conclusion, the threat of climate change to the Great Barrier Reef is profound and multifaceted. Rising ocean temperatures, ocean acidification, extreme weather events, and sea-level rise are all contributing to the decline of this iconic ecosystem. The impacts of climate change are already being felt across the reef, with widespread coral bleaching, loss of biodiversity, and degradation of marine habitats. While conservation efforts and scientific research offer hope for the future, the long-term survival of the Great Barrier Reef ultimately depends on global action to mitigate climate change. Without significant and sustained efforts to reduce greenhouse gas emissions, the future of the Great Barrier Reef remains uncertain, and one of the world's most extraordinary natural treasures could be lost forever.

Chapter 6: Protecting the Great Barrier Reef

Protecting the Great Barrier Reef for future generations is one of the most critical environmental challenges of our time. As the largest coral reef system on the planet, the Great Barrier Reef is not only a vibrant ecosystem teeming with marine life, but it also plays a crucial role in global biodiversity, climate regulation, and the livelihoods of millions of people. Spanning over 2,300 kilometers off the coast of Queensland, Australia, the reef is home to an astounding variety of species, including over 1,500 types of fish, more than 400 species of coral, and thousands of other marine organisms such as sharks, rays, mollusks, and sea turtles. Yet, despite its immense beauty and importance, the Great Barrier Reef faces unprecedented threats from human activities, particularly climate change, pollution, overfishing, and coastal development. The need to protect this natural wonder for future generations is urgent, and doing so requires a multi-faceted approach that involves government policies, scientific research, community involvement, and global cooperation.

One of the most pressing issues when it comes to protecting the Great Barrier Reef is mitigating the impacts of climate change, which poses the most significant long-term threat to the reef's survival. Rising ocean temperatures, driven by global warming, have led to widespread coral bleaching, where corals expel the symbiotic algae that live within their tissues and provide them with nutrients. Without these algae, corals turn white, or "bleach," and are left vulnerable to disease and death. Mass bleaching events have become alarmingly frequent in recent years, with severe occurrences in 2016, 2017, and 2020. During these events, large portions of the reef experienced significant coral mortality, particularly in the northern regions. The increasing frequency of bleaching is tied to marine heatwaves, which are becoming more common and intense as a result of climate change. If global temperatures continue to rise, the Great Barrier Reef may experience more frequent and severe bleaching events, putting its long-term survival at risk.

To protect the reef from the impacts of climate change, a global reduction in greenhouse gas emissions is essential. This requires collective action from governments, industries, and individuals worldwide to transition to cleaner energy sources and reduce the carbon footprint. The Paris Agreement, adopted in 2015, is an important step toward limiting global warming to well below 2 degrees Celsius, with an aspirational goal of keeping warming to 1.5 degrees Celsius above pre-industrial levels. Meeting these targets is critical for the survival of coral reefs like the Great Barrier Reef. Scientists have warned that warming beyond 1.5 degrees Celsius could lead to the loss of up to 90% of the world's coral reefs. Therefore, efforts to combat climate change through renewable energy, energy efficiency, carbon capture, and sustainable practices must be accelerated if we are to preserve the reef for future generations.

In addition to reducing emissions, local actions are also necessary to build the resilience of the Great Barrier Reef in the face of climate change. This includes improving water quality, as poor water quality exacerbates the impacts of climate change on the reef. Runoff from agricultural activities, particularly the use of fertilizers and pesticides, introduces harmful pollutants into the ocean, which can smother coral reefs, promote the growth of destructive algae, and weaken the overall health of the marine ecosystem. In response, efforts have been made to reduce the amount of sediment, nutrients, and chemicals entering the reef's waters. For instance, programs that encourage sustainable farming practices, such as reducing the use of chemical fertilizers, improving soil management, and preventing erosion, are essential to reducing agricultural runoff. These measures help maintain the health of the reef by ensuring that water quality is sufficient to support coral growth and resilience against environmental stressors.

Another vital aspect of protecting the Great Barrier Reef for future generations is the establishment of marine protected areas (MPAs) and the enforcement of regulations that safeguard the reef's ecosystems. The Great Barrier Reef Marine Park, established in 1975, is one of the largest and most well-known marine protected areas in the world. It covers approximately 344,400 square kilometers and is managed by the Great Barrier Reef Marine Park Authority (GBRMPA). The park is divided into different zones, each with specific rules regarding activities such as fishing, tourism, and scientific research. The zoning plan ensures that critical habitats, such as coral reefs, seagrass beds, and mangroves, are protected from harmful activities, while still allowing for sustainable use of the reef's resources.

MPAs like the Great Barrier Reef Marine Park play a crucial role in conserving biodiversity, maintaining ecosystem health, and promoting the recovery of species that have been overfished or otherwise impacted by human activities. By restricting harmful practices in certain areas, MPAs provide a refuge for marine life, allowing populations to recover and ecosystems to regenerate. However, while MPAs are an effective conservation tool, they must be complemented by strict enforcement and monitoring to ensure compliance with regulations. Illegal fishing, poaching, and other activities that damage the reef must be curbed through increased patrolling, surveillance, and community engagement. Involving local communities, particularly Indigenous groups who have lived in harmony with the reef for thousands of years, in the management and protection of the reef is also crucial. Indigenous knowledge and traditional practices can offer valuable insights into sustainable resource management and conservation efforts.

In addition to government-led initiatives and regulations, scientific research plays a fundamental role in protecting the Great Barrier Reef.

Ongoing research into the biology and ecology of coral reefs, as well as the development of new technologies and techniques, is essential for understanding the challenges facing the reef and finding innovative solutions. One such area of research is focused on coral restoration and resilience. Scientists are exploring ways to breed corals that are more resistant to heat stress and bleaching, which could help replenish damaged areas of the reef. For example, coral nurseries, where corals are grown in controlled environments before being transplanted back onto the reef, are being used to aid in reef restoration efforts. Additionally, researchers are studying the possibility of assisted gene flow, which involves moving corals with heat-tolerant genes to areas of the reef that are more vulnerable to bleaching.

Another promising avenue of research is the development of techniques to shade or cool sections of the reef during periods of extreme heat. This could involve the use of technologies such as cloud brightening, where fine particles are sprayed into the atmosphere to reflect sunlight and reduce sea surface temperatures. While these technologies are still in the experimental stage, they offer potential tools for mitigating the impacts of climate change on the reef in the short term while broader efforts to reduce global warming are pursued.

Public awareness and education are also key components of protecting the Great Barrier Reef for future generations. By increasing understanding of the importance of coral reefs and the threats they face, individuals can make more informed decisions about their own actions and advocate for stronger environmental policies. Educational programs aimed at schools, tourists, and the general public can foster a sense of stewardship and responsibility for the reef. Tourism operators, in particular, play a significant role in raising awareness among visitors to the reef. Many operators now incorporate environmental education into their tours, providing information about the reef's ecology, the challenges it faces, and how tourists can minimize their impact. Practices such as responsible snorkeling and diving, avoiding contact with corals, and adhering to designated pathways are simple but effective ways for visitors to help protect the reef while enjoying its beauty.

Tourism, when managed sustainably, can actually contribute to the protection of the Great Barrier Reef. The economic value of reef tourism provides a strong incentive for the Australian government and local communities to invest in its conservation. Sustainable tourism initiatives, such as eco-certification programs and green practices, encourage operators to minimize their environmental footprint while still providing a high-quality experience for visitors. This includes reducing carbon emissions, limiting waste, and supporting conservation projects. By aligning economic interests with environmental goals, sustainable tourism can play a positive role in reef protection.

However, tourism must be carefully managed to avoid contributing to the degradation of the reef. Unregulated or poorly managed tourism can lead to overcrowding, physical damage to coral reefs, and pollution. For this reason, it is essential that tourism activities are conducted in accordance with strict environmental guidelines and that tourism operators are held accountable for their environmental impact. Encouraging visitors to engage in responsible and sustainable behaviors, such as using reef-safe sunscreen and supporting conservation efforts, is a key part of ensuring that tourism contributes to the long-term health of the reef rather than its decline.

In addition to government policies, scientific research, and public education, global cooperation is necessary to protect the Great Barrier Reef for future generations. As a global issue, climate change requires a coordinated international response. Countries around the world must work together to reduce carbon emissions, invest in renewable energy, and develop strategies for adapting to the impacts of climate change. International organizations, such as the United Nations and the World Wildlife Fund (WWF), are actively involved in efforts to protect coral reefs worldwide, including the Great Barrier Reef. These organizations advocate for stronger environmental policies, provide funding for conservation projects, and raise global awareness of the importance of coral reefs. Collaborative efforts between governments, non-governmental organizations, scientists, and local communities are essential to developing effective strategies for reef conservation.

Protecting the Great Barrier Reef for future generations is not only a moral responsibility but also a practical necessity. The reef provides vital ecosystem services, including supporting fisheries, protecting coastlines from erosion and storms, and serving as a source of income for tourism and recreation. It is also a critical component of global biodiversity, hosting thousands of species that are found nowhere else on Earth. The loss of the Great Barrier Reef would have devastating consequences not only for marine life but also for human communities that depend on the reef for their livelihoods and cultural heritage.

The path to protecting the Great Barrier Reef for future generations is challenging, but it is not insurmountable. With concerted efforts to address climate change, reduce pollution, manage sustainable tourism, and invest in scientific research and restoration, it is possible to preserve this natural wonder for the enjoyment and benefit of generations to come. Each of us has a role to play, whether through individual actions, advocacy, or supporting policies that prioritize the health of our oceans. The time to act is now, before it is too late to save one of the world's most extraordinary ecosystems. The future of the Great Barrier Reef depends on our ability to work together, innovate, and make the necessary changes to ensure that this vibrant and vital ecosystem continues to thrive for centuries to come.

Chapter 7: Famous Shipwrecks Hidden in the Reef's Depths

The Great Barrier Reef, a natural marvel and the largest coral reef system in the world, has not only been a sanctuary for vibrant marine life but also a silent witness to countless historical events that unfolded on its treacherous waters. One of the most fascinating aspects of the reef's history is the numerous shipwrecks hidden in its depths, many of which are still being discovered and explored by divers and archaeologists. These shipwrecks, often the result of perilous navigation through the intricate maze of coral formations and shallow waters, hold immense historical significance, providing valuable insight into the maritime history of Australia and the world. Each wreck is a story frozen in time, a glimpse into the past that offers an intriguing combination of adventure, tragedy, and discovery.

The waters of the Great Barrier Reef have long been a challenging environment for sailors, particularly during the age of exploration and early maritime trade. Before the advent of modern navigation technologies, ships relied on rudimentary maps, compasses, and the skill of their crew to traverse the often unpredictable and dangerous waters of the reef. The sheer size of the reef, coupled with its ever-changing underwater topography, made it a notorious hazard for seafarers. Many ships, laden with precious cargo or passengers, met their fate when they collided with the jagged coral formations, were caught in sudden storms, or succumbed to navigational errors.

One of the most famous shipwrecks in the Great Barrier Reef is the wreck of HMS Pandora. The Pandora was a British Royal Navy ship dispatched in 1790 to capture the mutineers of the infamous HMS Bounty, who had taken control of the ship and fled to the Pacific after their rebellion against Captain William Bligh. The Pandora sailed across the South Pacific in search of the mutineers, eventually capturing

14 of them and imprisoning them in a makeshift cell onboard the ship known as "Pandora's Box." However, on its return voyage to England, the Pandora struck the Great Barrier Reef in August 1791. Despite efforts to free the ship, it quickly began to take on water and ultimately sank, taking 31 crew members and four prisoners with it. The rest of the crew and prisoners survived and managed to sail to safety using the ship's longboats.

The wreck of the Pandora was discovered in 1977 by marine archaeologists, and since then, it has become one of the most extensively studied and well-preserved shipwrecks in the reef. Numerous artifacts, including cannons, anchors, and personal items belonging to the crew and prisoners, have been recovered from the site, offering a rare glimpse into the daily lives of 18th-century sailors and the tragic events that led to the ship's demise. The Pandora wreck is not only an important archaeological site but also a reminder of the human drama and historical significance associated with the Great Barrier Reef.

Another notable shipwreck hidden within the reef's depths is the SS Yongala, a luxury passenger ship that met a tragic end in 1911. The Yongala was traveling from Melbourne to Cairns when it encountered a powerful cyclone off the coast of Queensland. Without any form of wireless communication on board, the ship was unable to receive warnings about the approaching storm, and it disappeared without a trace. All 122 passengers and crew on board perished in the disaster, making it one of Australia's deadliest maritime tragedies. For over half a century, the whereabouts of the Yongala remained a mystery, until it was finally discovered in 1958, lying intact on the ocean floor at a depth of approximately 30 meters near Cape Bowling Green.

Today, the SS Yongala is considered one of the world's best-preserved and most iconic shipwrecks, and it has become a popular dive site for adventurous divers from around the globe. The wreck has become a vibrant artificial reef, teeming with marine life such as giant groupers, sea turtles, rays, and a variety of colorful coral species that have colonized the remains of the ship. Diving the Yongala offers a unique opportunity to explore a piece of maritime history while experiencing the rich biodiversity of the Great Barrier Reef. The story of the Yongala is a haunting reminder of the dangers faced by early 20th-century maritime travelers and the powerful forces of nature that have shaped the reef's history.

The Great Barrier Reef is also home to many lesser-known but equally fascinating shipwrecks, each with its own unique story. One such wreck is the HMS Porpoise, a British naval vessel that ran aground on the reef in 1803. The Porpoise was part of an expedition led by Captain Matthew Flinders, who was returning to England after circumnavigating and mapping the coastline of Australia. Flinders, along with other members of the crew, managed to survive the wreck and were eventually rescued after a perilous journey to the mainland. The wreck of the Porpoise, like many others in the reef, serves as a testament to the challenges faced by early explorers as they ventured into uncharted waters.

Another intriguing wreck is that of the SS Gothenburg, a steamship that sank in 1875 after striking a coral reef while en route from Darwin to Adelaide. The ship was carrying gold bullion and important government documents, which added to the urgency of recovery efforts. However, despite attempts to salvage the gold, much of it was never recovered, and the wreck has since become shrouded in mystery and legend. The sinking of the Gothenburg claimed the lives of over 100 people, and the tragedy is still remembered as one of Australia's worst maritime disasters.

The shipwrecks of the Great Barrier Reef are not only significant for their historical value but also for their contribution to marine ecosystems. Over time, these wrecks have been transformed into thriving artificial reefs, providing shelter and habitat for a wide variety of marine species. The metal and wooden structures of the wrecks have been encrusted with corals, sponges, and algae, creating new ecosystems that attract fish, crustaceans, and other marine life. The wrecks offer a unique combination of history and marine biodiversity, making them important sites for both archaeologists and marine biologists.

In addition to the well-known wrecks, there are countless other shipwrecks scattered throughout the reef, many of which have yet to be discovered. The process of locating and documenting these wrecks is a challenging and time-consuming endeavor, requiring the use of advanced technologies such as sonar mapping, remotely operated vehicles (ROVs), and underwater imaging. However, each new discovery adds to our understanding of the maritime history of the Great Barrier Reef and the broader story of human exploration, trade, and settlement in the region.

Protecting these shipwrecks and their associated ecosystems is an important aspect of conserving the Great Barrier Reef. As more wrecks are discovered and explored, it is essential to ensure that they are preserved for future generations. This involves careful management of dive sites, protection against looting or unauthorized salvage, and ongoing scientific research to monitor the condition of the wrecks and the marine life that inhabits them.

The shipwrecks hidden within the depths of the Great Barrier Reef are not just remnants of a bygone era; they are living, evolving parts of the reef's complex ecosystem. Each wreck tells a story of human endeavor, exploration, and tragedy, while also serving as a testament to the power of nature and the resilience of life. The Great Barrier Reef, with its countless shipwrecks and vibrant marine life, continues to captivate the imagination of explorers, scientists, and divers, offering endless opportunities for discovery and wonder.

In conclusion, the famous shipwrecks hidden in the depths of the Great Barrier Reef are a rich tapestry of history, adventure, and marine biodiversity. From the tragic sinking of the HMS Pandora to the mysterious disappearance of the SS Yongala, these wrecks have become iconic symbols of the dangers and challenges faced by early mariners. Today, they serve as both archaeological treasures and thriving marine habitats, providing a unique window into the past and a vital resource for the future of the reef. The continued exploration and protection of these shipwrecks are essential to preserving the legacy of the Great Barrier Reef and ensuring that its stories can be shared with future generations.

Chapter 8: Sea Turtles and Their Role in the Reef Ecosystem

Sea turtles are among the most iconic and ancient marine creatures, having roamed the oceans for over 100 million years. They play a vital role in the delicate balance of the Great Barrier Reef's ecosystem. Their presence is not only a testament to the reef's biodiversity but also an essential component of the health and sustainability of the reef's complex web of life. These gentle reptiles contribute to the vitality of both marine and coastal ecosystems in a multitude of ways, influencing everything from the structure of seagrass beds to the health of coral reefs themselves. Understanding the significance of sea turtles in the reef ecosystem requires a deep dive into their behaviors, interactions with other species, and the critical roles they play in maintaining ecological equilibrium.

The Great Barrier Reef is home to six of the world's seven species of sea turtles: the green turtle, loggerhead turtle, hawksbill turtle, flatback turtle, olive ridley turtle, and leatherback turtle. Each of these species has unique habits and diets, but they all share an intrinsic connection to the reef and its surrounding environments. Sea turtles are migratory animals, traveling vast distances across the oceans, yet they often return to the same beaches where they were born to lay their eggs. This instinctive behavior links them to the health of both marine ecosystems, like coral reefs and seagrass meadows, as well as terrestrial ecosystems, like sandy beaches and dunes, where they lay their eggs.

One of the most important roles sea turtles play in the Great Barrier Reef is their contribution to the health of seagrass beds. Green turtles, in particular, are herbivorous and feed on seagrasses and algae. This grazing behavior helps to maintain the productivity and health of seagrass ecosystems. Seagrass beds are essential habitats for a variety of marine species, including fish, invertebrates, and other herbivores. By consuming the upper parts of seagrass blades, sea turtles prevent the seagrass from becoming overgrown and allow new shoots to grow. This natural "lawn-mowing" action encourages the growth of young, healthy seagrass, which is more nutrient-dense and productive. Without the grazing of sea turtles, seagrass beds could become overgrown, leading to a decrease in biodiversity and a reduction in the overall productivity of the ecosystem.

In addition to their influence on seagrass beds, sea turtles also play a crucial role in maintaining the health of coral reefs. Hawksbill turtles, for instance, feed primarily on sponges, which are abundant in coral reef environments. By consuming sponges, hawksbill turtles prevent them from overgrowing and outcompeting coral for space on the reef. This balance between sponges and coral is vital for the overall health of the reef, as it allows corals to flourish and maintain the structural integrity of the ecosystem. Without the presence of hawksbill turtles, sponges could proliferate and dominate the reef, leading to a decline in coral cover and a decrease in the biodiversity that relies on healthy coral structures.

Sea turtles also contribute to nutrient cycling within the reef ecosystem. As they graze on seagrasses and algae, sea turtles consume nutrients that are later redistributed throughout the reef in the form of waste. This nutrient cycling helps to fertilize both seagrass beds and coral reefs, promoting the growth of primary producers like algae and phytoplankton, which form the foundation of the marine food web. The presence of sea turtles in the reef system ensures that nutrients are efficiently recycled and redistributed, supporting the overall productivity of the ecosystem.

Beyond their direct interactions with seagrass and coral, sea turtles also play a role in the health of predator and prey dynamics within the reef. Sea turtles are preyed upon by a variety of species, including sharks and large fish. Juvenile turtles are particularly vulnerable to predation, and their presence in the food web supports the populations of these predators. At the same time, adult sea turtles can help control the populations of certain prey species, such as jellyfish. Leatherback turtles, for example, feed primarily on jellyfish, and their predation helps to regulate jellyfish populations in the reef. This balance between predator and prey is essential for maintaining the overall health and stability of the reef ecosystem.

Sea turtles also have a profound impact on the health of sandy beach and dune ecosystems, which are intricately connected to the reef. When sea turtles come ashore to lay their eggs, they play a role in nutrient transfer between the ocean and the land. Many of the eggs laid by sea turtles do not hatch, and the nutrients from these unhatched eggs contribute to the nutrient content of the surrounding sand and dunes. Additionally, hatchling sea turtles that do not survive provide food for terrestrial predators, such as crabs and birds. This nutrient transfer from the sea to the land is crucial for maintaining the health of coastal ecosystems, which, in turn, support the stability of the reef by preventing erosion and providing habitat for various species.

However, despite their importance to the Great Barrier Reef ecosystem, sea turtles face numerous threats, both natural and human-induced. Climate change is one of the most significant challenges, as rising ocean temperatures and changing sea levels can disrupt the delicate balance of the reef environment. Warmer ocean temperatures can affect the sex ratio of sea turtle hatchlings, as the temperature of the sand where eggs are incubated determines whether the hatchlings will be male or female. Higher temperatures often result in a higher proportion of female hatchlings, which can lead to skewed sex ratios and affect future populations.

Additionally, rising sea levels and increased storm frequency can destroy nesting beaches, making it difficult for sea turtles to find suitable places to lay their eggs. Coastal development, pollution, and plastic waste pose further threats to sea turtles, as they can become entangled in debris or mistake plastic for food, leading to injury or death. Overfishing and bycatch also threaten sea turtle populations, as turtles can become accidentally caught in fishing gear, leading to drowning or injury.

To protect sea turtles and their role in the Great Barrier Reef ecosystem, conservation efforts are critical. Marine protected areas, such as those established within the Great Barrier Reef Marine Park, help to safeguard important feeding and nesting habitats for sea turtles. Conservation programs that focus on reducing bycatch, protecting nesting beaches, and mitigating the impacts of climate change are essential for ensuring the long-term survival of these ancient reptiles. Public awareness campaigns and education initiatives can also play a role in reducing human impacts on sea turtles, encouraging responsible tourism practices, and promoting the reduction of plastic waste and pollution.

In conclusion, sea turtles are integral to the health and functioning of the Great Barrier Reef ecosystem. Their roles as grazers, predators, and nutrient cyclers contribute to the overall productivity and biodiversity of the reef. By maintaining the health of seagrass beds, controlling sponge populations, and regulating nutrient flows, sea turtles help to support the complex web of life that thrives in the reef's waters. However, the future of sea turtles and their role in the reef ecosystem is uncertain in the face of climate change and human activities. Protecting these magnificent creatures and their habitats is essential for preserving the Great Barrier Reef for future generations, ensuring that this natural wonder continues to thrive as one of the most vibrant and diverse ecosystems on Earth. Through concerted conservation efforts and global awareness, we can work to safeguard the future of sea turtles and the Great Barrier Reef they call home.

Chapter 9: Understanding Coral Bleaching and Its Effects

Coral bleaching is a phenomenon that has garnered significant attention in recent years due to its devastating impact on coral reefs, including the Great Barrier Reef. It is a process that occurs when corals, which are living organisms, expel the symbiotic algae (zooxanthellae) that live within their tissues. These algae are not only vital to the coral's health but also responsible for giving corals their vibrant colors. When corals are under stress, primarily due to environmental changes such as rising sea temperatures, they lose these algae, turning them white or "bleached." Although corals can survive for a short period in this state, prolonged bleaching can lead to their death, and the ripple effects extend throughout the entire ecosystem. Understanding the intricate process of coral bleaching, its triggers, and its far-reaching consequences is crucial to grasping the scale of the crisis facing coral reefs globally.

At the heart of coral bleaching is the relationship between corals and zooxanthellae. These microscopic algae live inside the coral's tissues and have a mutually beneficial partnership with their host. The zooxanthellae carry out photosynthesis, converting sunlight into energy, which they share with the coral. In return, the coral provides the algae with shelter and access to nutrients. This relationship is responsible for the incredible productivity and biodiversity of coral reefs, allowing corals to thrive in nutrient-poor tropical waters. The energy provided by the zooxanthellae enables corals to build the massive limestone structures that form the foundation of coral reefs, which in turn support thousands of species of marine life.

However, this symbiotic relationship is highly sensitive to changes in the environment. The most common trigger for coral bleaching is an increase in sea temperatures. When water temperatures rise, even by as little as 1-2 degrees Celsius above the normal seasonal maximum, it can cause the zooxanthellae to become stressed and produce toxic compounds. In response, the coral expels the algae to protect itself from further harm. Without the zooxanthellae, the coral loses its primary source of energy, and its tissues become transparent, revealing the white skeleton beneath. This is what gives bleached corals their stark, ghostly appearance.

While heat stress is the primary driver of coral bleaching, other factors can contribute to the phenomenon as well. Ocean acidification, caused by increased levels of carbon dioxide in the atmosphere, also plays a significant role in coral health. As the ocean absorbs more CO2, it becomes more acidic, which can weaken coral skeletons and reduce their ability to recover from bleaching events. Additionally, pollution, overfishing, and destructive fishing practices, such as blast fishing and cyanide fishing, can exacerbate the stress on coral reefs, making them more susceptible to bleaching.

The effects of coral bleaching are far-reaching and devastating, not only for the corals themselves but for the entire ecosystem that depends on them. When corals bleach, they lose their ability to perform essential functions such as building reef structures and providing habitat for marine species. Coral reefs are often referred to as the "rainforests of the sea" due to their incredible biodiversity. They support approximately 25% of all marine species, despite covering less than 1% of the ocean floor. The loss of corals due to bleaching threatens the survival of countless species, including fish, invertebrates, and marine mammals, many of which are directly dependent on healthy coral reefs for food, shelter, and breeding grounds.

The economic impact of coral bleaching is equally profound. Coral reefs provide substantial economic benefits to coastal communities and nations through tourism, fishing, and shoreline protection. In areas like the Great Barrier Reef, tourism associated with coral reefs generates billions of dollars in revenue each year. Healthy reefs attract tourists who come to snorkel, dive, and experience the vibrant marine life that coral reefs support. When bleaching occurs, the aesthetic and ecological value of reefs declines, leading to a decrease in tourism and associated economic activities. For many small island nations and coastal communities, the loss of coral reefs due to bleaching can have devastating consequences for their livelihoods and food security.

Fishing industries are also heavily reliant on coral reefs, which serve as important habitats for many commercially valuable fish species. As coral reefs decline due to bleaching, fish populations can diminish, leading to reduced catches and economic hardship for fishing communities. Moreover, the loss of coral reefs can disrupt the entire marine food web, as many fish species depend on coral reefs for part of their life cycle. The decline in fish populations can have a cascading effect on other marine predators and the overall health of the ocean.

Coral reefs also play a critical role in protecting coastlines from the damaging effects of storms and erosion. The complex structure of coral reefs acts as a natural barrier, absorbing the energy of waves and reducing the impact of storm surges on coastal areas. As coral reefs degrade due to bleaching, their ability to protect shorelines diminishes, leaving coastal communities more vulnerable to flooding and storm damage. This loss of natural protection can lead to increased costs for coastal infrastructure and disaster recovery efforts.

Despite the severity of coral bleaching, corals are resilient organisms that can recover from bleaching events if given enough time and if the stressors that caused the bleaching are removed. After expelling their zooxanthellae, corals can regain the algae and return to their normal state if water temperatures return to normal and other environmental conditions improve. However, the frequency and intensity of bleaching events have been increasing in recent years, giving corals less time to recover between events. This has led to widespread and long-term damage to coral reefs around the world.

The Great Barrier Reef, one of the most iconic and biodiverse coral reef systems on the planet, has experienced multiple mass bleaching events in recent decades. The most severe events occurred in 1998, 2002, 2016, 2017, and 2020, with each event affecting large portions of the reef. These bleaching events have led to significant coral mortality, with some areas of the reef losing up to 50% of their coral cover. The repeated bleaching of the Great Barrier Reef has raised concerns about the long-term survival of the reef and the species that depend on it.

Scientists and conservationists are working to address the issue of coral bleaching through a variety of strategies. One approach is to reduce the local stressors on coral reefs, such as pollution, overfishing, and destructive fishing practices. By improving the overall health of coral reef ecosystems, it is hoped that corals will be better able to withstand the stress of rising temperatures and other climate-related challenges. Marine protected areas (MPAs) are one tool that can help to safeguard coral reefs by restricting human activities in sensitive areas and promoting the recovery of damaged ecosystems.

Another approach is the development of coral restoration and rehabilitation techniques. These efforts involve the cultivation of coral fragments in nurseries and the replanting of corals onto degraded reefs. Researchers are also exploring the possibility of breeding or engineering "super corals" that are more resistant to heat stress and other environmental pressures. These resilient corals could be used to repopulate areas that have been severely impacted by bleaching. However, coral restoration efforts are still in their early stages and face significant challenges, including the scale of the problem and the difficulty of replicating the complex interactions that occur in natural coral reef ecosystems.

Ultimately, addressing the root cause of coral bleaching—climate change—will be essential to ensuring the long-term survival of coral reefs. Reducing greenhouse gas emissions and slowing the pace of global warming is critical to preventing further increases in sea temperatures and ocean acidification. International agreements such as the Paris Agreement aim to limit global temperature rise to below 2 degrees Celsius, but achieving these targets will require concerted efforts from governments, businesses, and individuals around the world. In addition to reducing emissions, efforts to mitigate the impacts of climate change, such as improving coastal resilience and protecting critical ecosystems, will be necessary to safeguard coral reefs and the communities that depend on them.

In conclusion, coral bleaching is a complex and multifaceted issue with far-reaching implications for marine ecosystems, coastal economies, and global biodiversity. The loss of coral reefs due to bleaching threatens the survival of countless species, disrupts marine food webs, and undermines the economic livelihoods of millions of people. While corals have the potential to recover from bleaching events, the increasing frequency and severity of these events pose a significant challenge to their survival. Protecting coral reefs from the effects of climate change and other environmental stressors will require a global effort to reduce emissions, improve conservation practices, and develop innovative solutions for coral restoration. The future of coral reefs, including the Great Barrier Reef, depends on our collective ability to address these challenges and safeguard these vital ecosystems for generations to come.

Chapter 10: The Great Barrier Reef as a World Heritage Site

The Great Barrier Reef, located off the northeastern coast of Australia, is one of the most iconic and significant natural wonders of the world. In 1981, it was designated as a World Heritage Site by UNESCO (United Nations Educational, Scientific and Cultural Organization), recognizing its outstanding universal value. Spanning over 2,300 kilometers and covering approximately 344,400 square kilometers, the Great Barrier Reef is the largest coral reef system on Earth, a title that emphasizes both its size and its global importance. Its designation as a World Heritage Site reflects not only its immense natural beauty but also its ecological, scientific, and cultural significance. To fully understand the importance of this status, it's essential to explore the reasons for its World Heritage designation, the biodiversity it harbors, the cultural and scientific value it holds, and the global efforts to protect and preserve it for future generations.

The Great Barrier Reef's World Heritage status is first and foremost based on its incredible biodiversity and unique ecosystems. This massive coral reef system supports an extraordinary range of marine species, many of which are found nowhere else on the planet. The reef is home to over 1,500 species of fish, more than 400 types of coral, and numerous species of sharks, rays, and other marine creatures. It is also a critical habitat for endangered and threatened species, such as dugongs and six of the world's seven species of marine turtles, including the green and loggerhead turtles. These turtles rely on the reef's sandy beaches and shallow waters for nesting, while dugongs feed on the seagrass beds found in the shallow coastal areas. The diverse ecosystems of the Great Barrier Reef support not only marine life but also a complex web of ecological interactions, making it a vital component of the broader marine environment.

Coral reefs, such as the Great Barrier Reef, are often referred to as the "rainforests of the sea" because of the rich biodiversity they support. Coral ecosystems are teeming with life, from microscopic plankton to large predatory fish, and they provide critical ecosystem services such as food, shelter, and breeding grounds for a wide range of species. Coral reefs are also intricately linked to other marine ecosystems, including mangroves and seagrass beds, which play essential roles in the life cycles of many marine organisms. The interconnectedness of these ecosystems highlights the Great Barrier Reef's importance not only as a coral reef but also as a hub of marine biodiversity that sustains life across vast stretches of the ocean.

In addition to its ecological value, the Great Barrier Reef holds immense scientific significance. As the largest living structure on Earth, it has been a focal point for marine research and environmental studies for decades. The reef provides scientists with unparalleled opportunities to study the complex dynamics of coral ecosystems, climate change impacts, marine biology, and oceanography. Coral reefs are particularly sensitive to environmental changes, making them valuable indicators of the health of the global marine environment. Researchers studying the Great Barrier Reef have contributed to our understanding of coral bleaching, ocean acidification, and the effects of rising sea temperatures on marine ecosystems. The reef's sheer scale and diversity make it a natural laboratory for studying the resilience and adaptability of marine life in the face of environmental challenges.

One of the most critical contributions of the Great Barrier Reef to science has been its role in understanding coral bleaching, a phenomenon in which corals expel the symbiotic algae (zooxanthellae) that live within their tissues. These algae provide the corals with energy through photosynthesis and give them their vibrant colors. When corals are stressed by environmental factors such as rising sea temperatures, they lose these algae, leading to the pale or white appearance known as bleaching. While corals can recover from bleaching if conditions improve, prolonged or repeated bleaching events can lead to coral death and the collapse of reef ecosystems. Research conducted on the Great Barrier Reef has been instrumental in highlighting the severity of coral bleaching and the urgent need for global action to address the causes of climate change, which is the primary driver of this phenomenon.

The cultural and indigenous significance of the Great Barrier Reef is another critical factor in its World Heritage status. For thousands of years, the reef has been integral to the lives of the Aboriginal and Torres Strait Islander peoples, who have lived in harmony with this vast ecosystem long before European settlement. These Indigenous groups have a deep spiritual and cultural connection to the reef, considering it a living entity that provides food, resources, and inspiration. Their knowledge of the reef and its ecosystems has been passed down through generations and continues to play a vital role in the management and conservation of the area. Traditional ecological knowledge, such as sustainable fishing practices and seasonal patterns, complements modern scientific research, helping to create a more holistic approach to reef management.

The designation of the Great Barrier Reef as a World Heritage Site underscores the global responsibility to protect and preserve this unique natural wonder. As a World Heritage Site, the reef is recognized as a place of "outstanding universal value," meaning it is not only important to Australia but to all of humanity. This status comes with international obligations to ensure the reef is preserved for future generations. Australia, as the custodian of the reef, has developed a comprehensive management plan to protect the reef, involving various stakeholders, including government agencies, Indigenous groups, scientists, and conservation organizations.

Despite its protected status, the Great Barrier Reef faces significant threats, with climate change being the most pressing. Rising sea temperatures, ocean acidification, and more frequent extreme weather events, such as cyclones, are all having a detrimental impact on the reef. The increased frequency and severity of coral bleaching events over the past few decades have been particularly alarming, with large portions of the reef experiencing significant bleaching in 2016, 2017, and 2020. These bleaching events have resulted in the loss of vast areas of coral cover, weakening the reef's ability to support marine life and perform its essential ecological functions.

In addition to climate change, other human activities pose threats to the reef, including coastal development, agricultural runoff, and overfishing. Sediment, pesticides, and nutrients from agricultural activities can run off into the ocean, causing water quality to deteriorate. This pollution can lead to outbreaks of coral-eating starfish, such as the crown-of-thorns starfish, which can decimate coral populations. Coastal development, including ports and shipping lanes, can also disrupt the natural balance of the reef's ecosystems, while overfishing can deplete key species that help maintain the health of the reef.

The Australian government, in partnership with conservation organizations and the international community, has taken numerous steps to address these threats and protect the reef. The Great Barrier Reef Marine Park Authority (GBRMPA) was established to manage and protect the reef, implementing zoning plans that regulate activities within the reef, such as fishing, tourism, and shipping. The GBRMPA works closely with scientists, Indigenous groups, and stakeholders to monitor the health of the reef and implement conservation strategies. Programs aimed at reducing agricultural runoff, controlling outbreaks of crown-of-thorns starfish, and promoting sustainable tourism practices are all part of the broader effort to preserve the reef.

In response to the growing threat of climate change, there has also been a concerted effort to mitigate the impacts of global warming on the reef. The Australian government has committed to reducing greenhouse gas emissions and supporting international agreements such as the Paris Agreement, which aims to limit global temperature rise to below 2 degrees Celsius. Additionally, innovative approaches to coral restoration and rehabilitation are being explored, including coral nurseries and the cultivation of heat-resistant coral species that may be more resilient to future climate challenges.

Public awareness and education play a vital role in the protection of the Great Barrier Reef. As a World Heritage Site, the reef attracts millions of visitors each year, providing an opportunity to educate people about the importance of coral reefs and the threats they face. Sustainable tourism practices are encouraged, and many tour operators work closely with conservation organizations to promote eco-friendly activities that minimize the impact on the reef. Educational programs and outreach initiatives, both in Australia and globally, aim to raise awareness of the importance of protecting coral reefs and inspire individuals to take action in their own lives to reduce their carbon footprint and support conservation efforts.

The Great Barrier Reef's World Heritage status has also made it a symbol of the global fight against climate change and environmental degradation. As one of the most visible and vulnerable natural wonders affected by climate change, the reef serves as a powerful reminder of the urgent need for global cooperation to protect the planet's ecosystems. It has become a rallying point for environmental activists, scientists, and policymakers advocating for stronger climate action and more robust environmental protection measures.

In conclusion, the Great Barrier Reef's designation as a World Heritage Site is a testament to its unparalleled natural beauty, ecological importance, and cultural significance. As the largest coral reef system in the world, it supports an extraordinary range of marine life, serves as a critical research site for scientists, and holds deep cultural value for Indigenous peoples. However, the reef is under threat from climate change, pollution, and human activities, making its protection an urgent global priority. The efforts to preserve the reef involve a complex web of conservation strategies, international cooperation, scientific research, and public awareness, all aimed at ensuring that this irreplaceable natural wonder remains a vibrant and thriving ecosystem for future generations to enjoy. The Great Barrier Reef, as a World Heritage Site, represents not only a marvel of nature but also a shared responsibility for the world to protect.

Chapter 11: Fun Facts About the Fish of the Great Barrier Reef

The fish of the Great Barrier Reef are among the most diverse and colorful inhabitants of the planet's largest coral reef system. The reef is home to over 1,500 species of fish, each playing a unique role in the reef's ecosystem and contributing to its dazzling underwater landscape. From the brightly colored parrotfish to the elusive and well-camouflaged stonefish, the variety of fish in the Great Barrier Reef is astonishing. These fish come in all shapes, sizes, and colors, with some species boasting incredible adaptations to life in the coral reef. As we explore fun facts about these fascinating fish, it becomes clear that they are not only essential to the health of the reef but also a source of endless wonder and discovery for marine enthusiasts and scientists alike.

One of the most iconic and easily recognizable fish species in the Great Barrier Reef is the clownfish, made famous by the animated movie *Finding Nemo*. Clownfish have a unique symbiotic relationship with sea anemones, which are stinging creatures that provide them with protection from predators. In return, clownfish clean the anemone and provide it with nutrients from their waste. Clownfish are born as males, and they have the ability to change their gender to female if necessary, a fascinating biological trait known as sequential hermaphroditism. If the dominant female of a clownfish group dies, the largest male will change sex and take her place as the new female. This adaptability ensures the survival of the species in changing environments.

Another fascinating fish found in the Great Barrier Reef is the parrotfish, named for its beak-like teeth that resemble a parrot's beak. Parrotfish are essential to the health of coral reefs because they feed on algae that grow on coral, preventing the algae from smothering the reef. As they munch on the algae, they also nibble on bits of coral, which they digest and excrete as sand. In fact, parrotfish are responsible for producing much of the fine white sand that covers tropical beaches. A single parrotfish can produce hundreds of pounds of sand each year. Parrotfish are also known for their striking colors, with vibrant hues of blue, green, pink, and yellow decorating their scales. Some species of parrotfish even sleep in a cocoon of mucus at night, which they secrete to protect themselves from predators.

The butterflyfish is another captivating species commonly seen in the Great Barrier Reef. These small, flat-bodied fish are named for their delicate, butterfly-like appearance and are often covered in intricate patterns and bright colors. Butterflyfish typically swim in pairs and are known for their monogamous behavior, with many pairs staying together for life. Their slender bodies and long snouts allow them to navigate the crevices of coral reefs, where they feed on small invertebrates and coral polyps. Their stunning colors and patterns, ranging from bold stripes to eye-like spots, serve as both camouflage and a defense mechanism to confuse predators.

One of the most well-camouflaged and potentially dangerous fish in the Great Barrier Reef is the stonefish. Stonefish are masters of disguise, blending perfectly with their surroundings by resembling a rock or a piece of coral. They are often hard to spot, even for experienced divers, due to their incredible ability to remain motionless for long periods. While stonefish may look harmless, they are one of the most venomous fish in the world. Their dorsal fins are equipped with sharp, venomous spines that can deliver a painful and potentially fatal sting to anyone who steps on or disturbs them. Despite their fearsome reputation, stonefish play a crucial role in the reef's ecosystem as ambush predators, feeding on small fish and crustaceans.

The Great Barrier Reef is also home to the majestic Napoleon wrasse, one of the largest reef fish, capable of growing up to 2 meters (6 feet) in length. This impressive fish is easily recognizable by the hump on its forehead and its vibrant green, blue, and purple colors.

The Napoleon wrasse is a gentle giant, known for its inquisitive nature and friendly interactions with divers. It plays a vital role in maintaining the health of the reef by feeding on toxic species, such as the crown-of-thorns starfish, which can cause significant damage to coral reefs if left unchecked. Despite its importance to the reef ecosystem, the Napoleon wrasse is listed as endangered due to overfishing and habitat loss.

The coral trout is another fascinating species that calls the Great Barrier Reef home. This predatory fish is highly prized by fishermen for its delicious meat, making it a popular target for both commercial and recreational fishing. Coral trout are known for their striking red or orange coloration, with black spots covering their bodies. These fish are ambush predators, lying in wait near coral outcrops before lunging at unsuspecting prey. Coral trout play a critical role in controlling populations of smaller reef fish, helping to maintain the balance of the ecosystem.

One of the most interesting fish behaviors in the Great Barrier Reef is the cleaning symbiosis exhibited by cleaner wrasses. These small fish set up cleaning stations where larger fish, such as groupers, moray eels, and even sharks, come to have parasites and dead skin removed from their bodies. The cleaner wrasse swims around and inside the mouths and gills of these larger fish, picking off parasites and cleaning wounds. In return, the larger fish allow the cleaner wrasse to feed without any threat of being eaten. This mutualistic relationship benefits both species and helps maintain the health of the reef's fish populations.

A unique species found in the deeper waters of the Great Barrier Reef is the flashlight fish. These small, nocturnal fish are known for the bioluminescent bacteria that live in special organs under their eyes, which produce a glowing light. Flashlight fish use this light to communicate with other members of their species, attract prey, and evade predators. The light can be turned on and off by rotating the glowing organ, making them appear to blink in the dark waters. This fascinating adaptation allows flashlight fish to thrive in the dimly lit areas of the reef, where they hunt for small crustaceans and plankton at night.

The Great Barrier Reef is also home to several species of damselfish, which are small, territorial fish known for their bold personalities and vibrant colors. Damselfish play a vital role in maintaining the health of coral reefs by farming algae, which they feed on. They aggressively defend their algae gardens from other fish and even from divers who get too close. Despite their small size, damselfish are known for their feisty behavior, often chasing away fish much larger than themselves to protect their territory. Some species of damselfish are also known for their unique courtship displays, in which males build and defend nests of algae to attract females.

Another fascinating inhabitant of the Great Barrier Reef is the lionfish, an exotic-looking predator with long, venomous spines that radiate from its body like a lion's mane. Lionfish are native to the Indo-Pacific region, including the Great Barrier Reef, but have become an invasive species in other parts of the world, such as the Atlantic Ocean. In the reef, lionfish are ambush predators, feeding on small fish and invertebrates. Their venomous spines provide them with protection from predators, while their striking red, white, and brown stripes help them blend in with the coral. Despite their beauty, lionfish are dangerous to humans, as their venom can cause extreme pain and swelling.

The goby is another interesting fish species that can be found in the Great Barrier Reef. Gobies are small, bottom-dwelling fish that often form symbiotic relationships with shrimp. The shrimp digs and maintains a burrow in the sand, which both the shrimp and the goby share as a home. In return, the goby keeps watch for predators and alerts the shrimp to any danger by flicking its tail. This unique partnership benefits both the goby and the shrimp, allowing them to coexist in a mutually beneficial relationship that helps them survive in the reef's complex environment.

The Great Barrier Reef is also home to several species of sharks, including the blacktip reef shark, whitetip reef shark, and the larger tiger shark. Reef sharks are an essential part of the coral reef ecosystem, acting as apex predators that help regulate the populations of smaller fish and maintain the balance of the food chain. Despite their fearsome reputation, reef sharks are generally not a threat to humans and are often seen swimming gracefully through the coral gardens of the reef. These sharks play a crucial role in keeping the reef's ecosystem healthy by controlling fish populations and preventing any one species from becoming too dominant.

In conclusion, the fish of the Great Barrier Reef are not only incredibly diverse but also play essential roles in maintaining the health and balance of the reef's ecosystem. From the algae-grazing parrotfish to the predatory lionfish, each species has adapted to life in this vibrant underwater world in unique and fascinating ways. Whether through symbiotic relationships, camouflage, or specialized feeding habits, the fish of the Great Barrier Reef contribute to the overall health and resilience of the reef. Their diversity and adaptability make them a key component of one of the most complex and beautiful ecosystems on Earth.

Chapter 12: The Role of Sharks in Keeping the Reef Balanced

Sharks play a crucial role in maintaining the delicate balance of the Great Barrier Reef ecosystem. As apex predators, sharks are at the top of the food chain and exert a powerful influence on the populations of other marine species. Their presence helps regulate the numbers of smaller predatory fish, herbivores, and other creatures, which in turn impacts the health and survival of coral reefs. Without sharks, the intricate relationships between species in the reef could spiral out of control, leading to devastating consequences for the entire ecosystem.

One of the most important roles sharks fulfill in the Great Barrier Reef is controlling the population of mid-level predators. These predators, such as groupers and snappers, feed on herbivorous fish like parrotfish and surgeonfish. These herbivores play a vital role in the reef ecosystem by grazing on algae that grow on the surface of coral. If the populations of herbivorous fish were to decline due to over-predation by mid-level predators, algae would quickly overgrow the coral, suffocating it and preventing new coral growth. Sharks, by keeping the numbers of mid-level predators in check, help ensure that the herbivorous fish populations remain healthy, which is essential for the survival of the coral.

Sharks also play a role in keeping the populations of weaker or sick fish in check. By preying on the slower or less healthy members of fish populations, sharks help maintain the genetic strength of fish communities. This natural selection process ensures that only the fittest individuals survive and reproduce, which strengthens the overall resilience of species in the reef. A healthy population of sharks can therefore promote healthier fish stocks, which in turn supports the health of the entire reef ecosystem. Without this regulation, weaker and sickly fish could overpopulate, leading to a decline in overall species fitness and an increase in disease transmission.

Sharks also contribute to the health of coral reefs through a phenomenon known as the "fear effect." This refers to the behavior changes that prey species exhibit when they know that sharks are nearby. The mere presence of sharks can alter the feeding habits and movements of other species, particularly mid-level predators and herbivores. For example, when sharks are present, herbivorous fish may graze more cautiously, moving between different areas of the reef rather than overgrazing one section. This creates a more even distribution of grazing pressure, preventing any single area of coral from being stripped of its algae. By spreading out the grazing activity, sharks help protect the structural integrity and biodiversity of the reef.

Interestingly, sharks are not just passive regulators of the reef ecosystem—they actively shape the habitats within it. Some species of sharks, such as the blacktip reef shark and the whitetip reef shark, are known to patrol specific territories within the reef, and their hunting activity can impact the distribution of other species within these areas. By targeting specific prey in certain regions, sharks can indirectly influence the population dynamics of entire reef communities. In some cases, sharks' territorial behavior may also lead to the creation of "no-go" zones for certain prey species, allowing some areas of the reef to serve as refuges where smaller fish and invertebrates can thrive without constant predation pressure.

Different species of sharks serve different roles within the reef, each contributing uniquely to the balance of the ecosystem. For example, reef sharks like the blacktip reef shark, whitetip reef shark, and grey reef shark are typically smaller than open-ocean species like tiger sharks or bull sharks, but they are no less important. These reef-dwelling sharks tend to focus on smaller prey such as fish, octopuses, and crustaceans, while larger species like tiger sharks may hunt larger animals like sea turtles or even other sharks. This division of labor among shark species ensures that no single prey group is over-predated, which helps maintain the balance of different species within the reef.

Sharks also play an essential role in nutrient cycling within the reef ecosystem. When sharks feed on their prey, they release nutrients into the water through excretion, which can be absorbed by plankton and other organisms lower down the food chain. This process helps maintain nutrient availability in the water column, supporting the growth of phytoplankton and other microscopic organisms that form the base of the marine food web. In addition, when sharks die naturally, their bodies decompose and provide nutrients for scavengers and decomposers in the reef, further contributing to nutrient cycling.

Another interesting aspect of sharks' influence on the Great Barrier Reef is their contribution to maintaining the health of seagrass beds, which are often found adjacent to coral reefs. Large sharks like tiger sharks help protect seagrass beds by preying on herbivores such as dugongs and green sea turtles. These herbivores feed on seagrass, and without predators like sharks to regulate their populations, they could overgraze seagrass beds, leading to their degradation. Healthy seagrass beds are important for the overall health of the reef, as they serve as nursery grounds for many marine species and help stabilize the seafloor, reducing the amount of sediment that could smother coral reefs.

In addition to their ecological roles, sharks are also important indicators of the overall health of the reef. Because sharks are apex predators, their populations are often affected by changes lower down the food chain. Declining shark numbers can signal that something is wrong in the ecosystem, such as overfishing, habitat destruction, or pollution. Conversely, healthy shark populations indicate that the reef's food web is functioning properly and that the ecosystem is in balance. Sharks, therefore, serve as a barometer for the overall health of coral reef ecosystems like the Great Barrier Reef.

However, sharks face numerous threats that can disrupt their role in the reef. Overfishing, both targeted and as bycatch, has led to declines in shark populations worldwide, including in the Great Barrier Reef. Sharks are particularly vulnerable to overfishing because they have slow growth rates, long gestation periods, and produce relatively few offspring compared to other fish. As a result, even small reductions in shark populations can have significant and long-lasting effects on the reef ecosystem. The loss of sharks from the reef could lead to unchecked populations of mid-level predators, which would, in turn, lead to a decline in herbivorous fish and an increase in algae overgrowth on the coral.

Another major threat to sharks is habitat degradation, particularly from coral bleaching events caused by rising ocean temperatures. When coral reefs suffer from bleaching, they lose the complex structure that provides shelter and hunting grounds for sharks and their prey. This can lead to a decline in prey availability for sharks, forcing them to either move to less suitable habitats or face starvation. In some cases, sharks may also be more vulnerable to fishing pressures when their habitats are degraded, as they may be forced into more open waters where they are more easily caught.

Sharks are also affected by pollution, particularly plastic pollution and chemical contaminants. Plastic waste in the ocean can entangle sharks, restricting their movement and leading to injury or death. Additionally, sharks may mistake plastic debris for food, ingesting it and suffering from blockages or internal injuries. Chemical pollutants, such as heavy metals and pesticides, can accumulate in sharks' bodies over time, leading to health problems and reduced reproductive success. These threats, combined with the broader impacts of climate change, pose significant challenges for the future of shark populations in the Great Barrier Reef.

Conservation efforts to protect sharks are critical for ensuring the long-term health of the Great Barrier Reef. Marine protected areas (MPAs) within the reef help safeguard shark habitats from overfishing and other human activities, providing safe zones where sharks can thrive and fulfill their ecological roles. In addition, shark conservation programs focused on reducing bycatch, promoting sustainable fishing practices, and raising awareness about the importance of sharks in the ecosystem can help reduce the pressures on shark populations. Research and monitoring programs are also essential for understanding the status of shark populations and identifying areas where conservation efforts are most needed.

In conclusion, sharks are essential to the balance of the Great Barrier Reef ecosystem. As apex predators, they regulate the populations of other species, control the spread of disease, and maintain the health of coral reefs through their influence on prey behavior and habitat use. Sharks contribute to nutrient cycling, protect seagrass beds, and serve as indicators of ecosystem health. However, sharks face numerous threats from overfishing, habitat degradation, and pollution, all of which can disrupt their role in the reef. Protecting sharks is crucial for the continued health and resilience of the Great Barrier Reef, ensuring that this vibrant ecosystem can thrive for generations to come.

Chapter 13: Snorkeling Adventures in the Waters of the Reef

Snorkeling in the Great Barrier Reef is one of the most captivating and exhilarating ways to experience the vibrant and colorful underwater world of this extraordinary natural wonder. For those who seek adventure and a deep connection with marine life, snorkeling offers an accessible and awe-inspiring journey through crystal-clear waters teeming with an incredible array of sea creatures, coral formations, and hidden treasures. As you float gently on the surface, looking down into the depths, you are treated to a dazzling display of life in one of the most biodiverse ecosystems on the planet.

The Great Barrier Reef, stretching over 2,300 kilometers along the coast of Queensland, Australia, is home to a kaleidoscope of coral species, each more breathtaking than the last. Snorkelers have the unique opportunity to witness these corals up close, marveling at their complex structures and the myriad colors that seem to shift and change with the light. The coral formations are not just visually stunning; they also provide shelter and sustenance for countless species of fish, crustaceans, and other marine creatures. As you snorkel through the reef, you can see these animals darting in and out of the coral, creating a bustling, vibrant underwater community that feels alive with energy and movement.

One of the most thrilling aspects of snorkeling in the Great Barrier Reef is the sheer diversity of fish that inhabit its waters. From the brightly colored clownfish hiding among the waving tentacles of sea anemones to the sleek, shimmering parrotfish munching on coral, the reef is home to thousands of different species, each with its own unique appearance and behavior. Schools of tiny, glittering fish often swim in unison, creating mesmerizing patterns as they move in perfect harmony. Larger species, such as groupers or wrasses, may glide by slowly, their powerful bodies moving gracefully through the water. For those lucky enough to spot them, encounters with larger marine creatures like sea turtles, rays, or even the occasional reef shark are unforgettable moments that can turn a snorkeling trip into a once-in-a-lifetime experience.

The waters of the Great Barrier Reef are known for their remarkable clarity, especially in the outer reef regions, where visibility can sometimes exceed 20 meters. This exceptional clarity allows snorkelers to enjoy unobstructed views of the reef's underwater landscapes, from shallow coral gardens to deep drop-offs that plunge into the ocean's depths. The sensation of floating above such a vast, vibrant world, with nothing but water between you and the reef below, is both peaceful and exhilarating. The gentle ebb and flow of the tides create a rhythmic motion that carries you along as you explore, making the experience feel almost dreamlike.

As you snorkel along the surface, you may come across vast coral bommies—large, dome-shaped coral formations that rise up from the seafloor like underwater mountains. These bommies are often teeming with life, providing a perfect vantage point for observing a wide variety of marine species. Around the edges of the bommies, you'll see a myriad of coral types, including brain coral, staghorn coral, and the majestic plate coral, which creates vast, layered structures that seem to go on forever. Soft corals, which sway gently with the current, add even more variety to the reefscape, their delicate branches creating an ethereal, almost otherworldly atmosphere.

In addition to the corals and fish, the Great Barrier Reef is home to a wide array of fascinating invertebrates, many of which are easily spotted while snorkeling. Sea stars, or starfish, come in a variety of shapes, sizes, and colors, and can often be seen clinging to rocks or slowly moving across the seabed in search of food. Sea cucumbers, which may look strange to human eyes, play an important role in the reef's ecosystem by helping to clean the sand and recycle nutrients.

Spiny lobsters, with their long, delicate antennae, hide in the crevices of the reef, while giant clams, some of which can grow up to a meter in length, sit nestled in the coral, their colorful mantles visible as they filter-feed on plankton.

Perhaps one of the most exciting and sought-after experiences for snorkelers in the Great Barrier Reef is the chance to swim with sea turtles. These ancient and gentle creatures are often spotted gliding effortlessly through the water, their slow, graceful movements making them a joy to observe. The Great Barrier Reef is home to several species of sea turtles, including the green sea turtle, hawksbill turtle, and loggerhead turtle. These turtles often frequent the shallow waters of the reef, where they feed on seagrass beds and algae. Watching a sea turtle up close, especially as it ascends to the surface for a breath of air before diving back down to continue its peaceful journey, is a magical experience that leaves a lasting impression.

Snorkeling in the Great Barrier Reef also provides the opportunity to witness the fascinating interactions between different species. Cleaner fish, for example, play a vital role in the reef's ecosystem by removing parasites and dead skin from larger fish. As you snorkel, you may see cleaner wrasse or cleaner shrimp darting around larger fish, performing this important service. Watching this symbiotic relationship in action is just one of the many ways that snorkeling reveals the complexity and interconnectedness of life on the reef.

For those looking for even more adventure, certain areas of the Great Barrier Reef offer the opportunity to snorkel around shipwrecks. These wrecks, now colonized by coral and marine life, add an extra layer of mystery and excitement to a snorkeling trip. The coral that has grown over these man-made structures creates a rich and varied habitat for marine creatures, and exploring these underwater relics is a thrilling way to combine history with natural beauty. As you swim over the wreckage, you can imagine the stories of the ships that once sailed these waters, now transformed into vibrant ecosystems that are teeming with life.

While snorkeling is often seen as a peaceful and relaxing activity, there are moments of pure excitement, especially when larger marine animals make an appearance. Snorkelers might find themselves in the company of manta rays, whose enormous wingspans and elegant movements make them one of the most majestic creatures of the reef. Manta rays are known for their graceful, acrobatic swimming, and watching them glide effortlessly through the water is a breathtaking experience. In deeper areas of the reef, snorkelers may also spot reef sharks or even the occasional hammerhead shark. While the idea of swimming with sharks might seem intimidating, these creatures are generally harmless to humans and are more interested in hunting fish than interacting with snorkelers. Seeing a shark in its natural habitat, moving with power and purpose, is a reminder of the awe-inspiring diversity and strength of the reef's ecosystem.

One of the joys of snorkeling in the Great Barrier Reef is the sense of discovery that comes with each new dive. No two snorkeling experiences are ever the same, as the reef is constantly changing with the tides, weather, and the movements of its inhabitants. One day, you might encounter a playful pod of dolphins swimming nearby, while another might bring a close encounter with a stingray gliding along the seafloor. The unpredictable and ever-changing nature of the reef makes each snorkeling trip a unique and unforgettable adventure.

Snorkeling also offers an unparalleled opportunity to observe the smaller, often overlooked creatures that inhabit the reef. Nudibranchs, also known as sea slugs, are a favorite among snorkelers for their vibrant colors and intricate patterns. These tiny, soft-bodied creatures come in an astonishing variety of shapes and sizes, and spotting one among the corals is like discovering a hidden treasure. Similarly, the reef is home to countless species of small crustaceans, such as crabs and shrimp, which can often be seen scuttling along the sandy seafloor or hiding in the crevices of the coral. Observing these tiny creatures up close gives snorkelers a deeper appreciation for the reef's immense biodiversity and the delicate balance that sustains it.

One of the best times to snorkel in the Great Barrier Reef is during the annual coral spawning event, which typically occurs in late spring or early summer. This natural phenomenon, often described as an underwater snowstorm, sees millions of coral polyps releasing their eggs and sperm into the water in a synchronized spawning event. The sight of the water filled with tiny pink and white particles, drifting through the currents, is a truly magical experience. Snorkelers who are fortunate enough to witness this event are treated to one of nature's most extraordinary spectacles, as the reef comes alive with new life.

In conclusion, snorkeling in the crystal-clear waters of the Great Barrier Reef offers an unparalleled adventure that immerses you in the beauty and wonder of one of the world's most biodiverse ecosystems. From the vibrant corals and colorful fish to the majestic sea turtles and graceful rays, every moment spent snorkeling in the reef is filled with excitement, discovery, and awe. Whether you are a seasoned snorkeler or a first-time visitor, the Great Barrier Reef promises an unforgettable journey into the heart of the ocean's most vibrant and thriving ecosystem, where every glance beneath the surface reveals a world of wonder waiting to be explored.

Chapter 14: The History of Indigenous Peoples and the Reef

The history of Indigenous peoples and the Great Barrier Reef is a story that spans thousands of years, showcasing a deep and enduring connection between Australia's First Nations communities and the natural environment, particularly the vast, intricate ecosystem of the reef. Indigenous peoples, specifically the Aboriginal and Torres Strait Islander groups, have lived alongside the Great Barrier Reef for at least 60,000 years, long before European explorers ever set sail for Australia. Their knowledge of the reef and its resources, developed through generations of lived experience, oral tradition, and cultural practices, is an essential part of understanding the historical significance of the reef, not only as a natural wonder but also as a cultural and spiritual landscape.

For the Aboriginal and Torres Strait Islander peoples, the Great Barrier Reef is far more than a natural resource or a place of beauty. It holds profound cultural, spiritual, and social meaning. The reef and the surrounding waters are considered a living entity, with their own stories, ancestors, and totems. These Indigenous groups have complex Dreaming stories that describe the creation of the reef, the islands, and the marine life that inhabit it. Dreaming, or "Tjukurpa" in some Aboriginal languages, is a central concept in Aboriginal culture, referring to the spiritual, cultural, and physical connection to the land and sea. These stories are passed down through generations and explain the origins of the land and sea, the creatures within them, and the responsibilities of people to care for their environment.

One such Dreaming story from the Wuthathi people of Cape York Peninsula explains how their ancestral spirits shaped the reef. According to their oral traditions, a large snake, known as the Rainbow Serpent, traveled through the region and created the reef, as well as the rivers and mountains. These stories provide a spiritual framework for understanding the environment, and they also offer valuable ecological insights into how Indigenous people have sustainably managed the reef for millennia. The Rainbow Serpent is considered a protector of the natural world, and the story conveys the message that people must respect and care for the land and sea to ensure its continued vitality.

The Torres Strait Islanders, who live on the islands between the northern tip of Queensland and Papua New Guinea, have similarly rich cultural traditions that are deeply intertwined with the reef. For these seafaring people, the reef has provided sustenance, shelter, and spiritual guidance for thousands of years. The waters surrounding the Torres Strait Islands are rich in marine life, and fishing has always been a central part of their way of life. They developed sophisticated fishing techniques and tools, which were passed down through generations. Dugout canoes, spears, and fish traps made from natural materials are examples of the traditional technologies that allowed Torres Strait Islanders to harvest fish, turtles, and other marine creatures sustainably. These practices were not only about survival but were also tied to cultural rituals, stories, and beliefs that governed how and when certain animals could be harvested.

Indigenous peoples' connection to the reef is not just about physical sustenance but also about maintaining balance and harmony with the natural world. They understood the importance of conserving the resources of the reef, ensuring that the ecosystem remained healthy and abundant for future generations. This knowledge, often referred to as Traditional Ecological Knowledge (TEK), encompasses not only the practical aspects of living off the land and sea but also a deep understanding of the ecological processes that sustain the reef. Indigenous peoples were among the first environmental stewards, practicing sustainable fishing, hunting, and gathering methods long before modern conservation efforts emerged. Their seasonal calendars, based on the cycles of nature, informed when to hunt, fish, or harvest certain plants and animals, ensuring that species were not overexploited.

Indigenous marine management practices were, and still are, deeply tied to cultural law. In many Aboriginal cultures, land and sea are not seen as separate entities but are instead interconnected parts of a whole. The ocean is as much a part of their country as the land, and the reef is viewed as an integral part of their ancestral homeland. This is why Indigenous peoples often refer to "Sea Country," a term that encapsulates the idea that the sea and its resources are part of their cultural landscape. Sea Country includes not just the physical features of the ocean, such as coral reefs, seagrass beds, and mangroves, but also the cultural and spiritual connections that Indigenous peoples have with the sea.

The Indigenous peoples of the Great Barrier Reef region also developed complex systems of governance and stewardship over their Sea Country. These systems were based on kinship, clan groups, and spiritual beliefs, and they governed how resources were used, who had access to certain areas, and how to ensure that the environment was cared for. Elders and other community leaders played a key role in teaching younger generations about the responsibilities they had to the land and sea, passing on knowledge about fishing, hunting, and caring for sacred sites. The practice of "firestick farming," a method of using controlled burns to manage the landscape, is one example of how Indigenous peoples applied their knowledge to shape the environment in ways that promoted biodiversity and reduced the risk of larger, uncontrollable fires. While firestick farming is more commonly associated with terrestrial ecosystems, it reflects the broader Indigenous philosophy of land management that also extends to marine environments.

Despite the long and rich history of Indigenous peoples and their connection to the Great Barrier Reef, the arrival of European settlers in the late 18th century brought profound and often devastating changes.

The colonization of Australia resulted in the displacement of Indigenous peoples from their lands and waters, the destruction of traditional ways of life, and the imposition of European legal systems that disregarded Indigenous law and governance. Indigenous communities were often pushed to the margins of society, and their traditional knowledge and practices were undervalued or outright ignored by colonial authorities. In the case of the Great Barrier Reef, this led to the exploitation of marine resources and the degradation of the environment, as European settlers viewed the reef as a resource to be exploited for economic gain.

The colonization of the region also introduced new threats to the reef, including overfishing, pollution, and the introduction of invasive species. Indigenous peoples, who had long viewed the reef as a source of spiritual and cultural sustenance, were largely excluded from decision-making processes that affected the management and conservation of the reef. The imposition of European land ownership systems, including the declaration of marine parks and protected areas, often ignored the rights and interests of Indigenous peoples, further marginalizing their role in the stewardship of the reef.

However, in recent decades, there has been a growing recognition of the importance of Indigenous knowledge and leadership in the management of the Great Barrier Reef. Indigenous Land and Sea Ranger programs have been established, allowing Aboriginal and Torres Strait Islander communities to take an active role in managing their Sea Country. These programs empower Indigenous peoples to use their traditional knowledge alongside modern scientific practices to protect and conserve the reef. Indigenous rangers work to monitor the health of the reef, manage the impacts of climate change, and protect important cultural sites. This collaboration between Indigenous communities and government agencies represents an important step toward recognizing the rights of Indigenous peoples to manage their traditional lands and waters and ensuring that the reef is protected for future generations.

In 1981, the Great Barrier Reef was inscribed on the UNESCO World Heritage List, in part because of its cultural significance to Indigenous peoples. The World Heritage listing acknowledges that the reef is not only an extraordinary natural wonder but also a cultural landscape that has been shaped by the knowledge, practices, and beliefs of the region's Indigenous peoples. Efforts to incorporate Indigenous voices into the management of the reef continue to grow, with initiatives such as co-management agreements and the inclusion of Indigenous knowledge in conservation planning.

Today, Indigenous peoples continue to advocate for their rights to Sea Country and work to protect the reef for future generations. Their deep connection to the reef, forged over thousands of years, is a testament to their resilience and their enduring role as stewards of one of the world's most iconic ecosystems. As the Great Barrier Reef faces unprecedented challenges from climate change, pollution, and other human activities, the knowledge and leadership of Indigenous peoples will be crucial in ensuring that the reef remains healthy and vibrant for generations to come. Understanding the history of Indigenous peoples and the reef is not only about acknowledging the past but also about recognizing the vital role they play in shaping the future of this precious ecosystem.

Chapter 15: Diving Deep: Exploring the Reef's Hidden Caves

Diving deep into the Great Barrier Reef's hidden caves is an extraordinary adventure that takes explorers into the mysterious and lesser-known corners of this vast underwater world. While the vibrant corals and colorful marine life on the surface of the reef are well known, the intricate network of caves, crevices, and tunnels beneath the water's surface holds its own unique wonders. These hidden caves are not only geological marvels but also serve as crucial habitats for a diverse array of marine species, offering a glimpse into an ancient and still largely unexplored world. For divers and scientists alike, the exploration of these submerged cave systems presents an opportunity to discover rare and elusive creatures, gain a better understanding of reef dynamics, and experience the awe-inspiring beauty of one of nature's most complex ecosystems.

The Great Barrier Reef's caves were formed over millions of years, shaped by the natural processes of erosion and coral growth. These caves are made primarily of limestone, which is formed from the skeletons of dead marine organisms such as coral polyps and other calcium-carbonate-producing creatures. Over time, the accumulation of these skeletal remains creates large structures that, combined with the movements of the sea and the shifting of tectonic plates, lead to the formation of intricate cave systems. The constant ebb and flow of ocean currents, as well as the chemical action of slightly acidic water dissolving the limestone, gradually carve out caves, tunnels, and crevices that stretch deep into the heart of the reef.

Exploring these underwater caves is a challenge, even for experienced divers, as they require specialized skills and equipment. The confined spaces, low visibility, and the presence of potentially dangerous marine life make cave diving a highly technical and sometimes risky endeavor. Divers must be equipped with proper lighting, backup oxygen supplies, and advanced navigation tools to ensure they can safely navigate the labyrinth of passages. Despite the difficulties, the rewards of diving into these caves are immense. Many of the creatures that inhabit the deeper sections of the reef cannot be found in the shallower waters. These caves serve as sanctuaries for rare fish, invertebrates, and other marine organisms that are specially adapted to the dark, cool environments found within the caves.

One of the most fascinating aspects of the Great Barrier Reef's hidden caves is the abundance of marine life that thrives in these secluded environments. While the reef itself is teeming with life, from tiny shrimp to massive sea turtles, the caves are home to more elusive and specialized species. In the darkness of the caves, bioluminescent organisms light up the walls with a magical glow, creating an otherworldly ambiance that is unlike anything seen in the sunlit sections of the reef. Creatures such as flashlight fish, which use bioluminescence to communicate and attract prey, can often be found in the depths of these caves, their glowing bodies creating a mesmerizing spectacle as they dart through the dark waters.

Another group of creatures that make their homes in the caves of the reef are the various species of sharks and rays. Sharks, particularly reef sharks and white-tip sharks, often use the caves as resting places during the day. These nocturnal hunters are known to retreat to the safety and shelter of the caves, where they can rest undisturbed until nightfall, when they emerge to hunt in the open waters of the reef. The caves provide these apex predators with a secure habitat where they can escape from potential threats and conserve energy. Similarly, rays, including the graceful manta rays and stingrays, can sometimes be found gliding silently through the tunnels, their large wingspans effortlessly navigating the narrow spaces.

Apart from the larger marine life, the caves are also teeming with smaller creatures that are rarely seen outside of these environments.

Various species of crustaceans, including crabs, lobsters, and shrimp, hide in the nooks and crannies of the cave walls, using the darkness and the complex structures as protection from predators. Spiny lobsters, for example, are commonly found in the caves, their long antennae extending outward as they search for food in the safety of their rocky hideouts. Other invertebrates, such as brittle stars and sea cucumbers, can also be found clinging to the cave walls, feeding on organic material that drifts through the water.

One of the most striking features of the caves is the diversity of corals that thrive in these shadowy environments. While corals are often associated with the bright, sunlit waters of the reef's surface, many species have adapted to life in the dimly lit caves. These corals, often called "cave corals" or "deep-water corals," are typically less reliant on sunlight than their shallow-water counterparts. Instead of photosynthesizing, these corals derive their energy from filtering nutrients out of the water. The unique water currents that flow through the caves bring a steady supply of plankton and other organic matter, which these corals can capture using their specialized polyps. This adaptation allows corals to colonize even the darkest corners of the reef's cave systems, creating a beautiful yet eerie underwater landscape of coral formations that resemble stalactites and stalagmites in a terrestrial cave.

Cave diving in the Great Barrier Reef is also an opportunity to witness the intricate geology of the reef. The caves offer a unique cross-section of the reef's structure, revealing layers of coral skeletons and limestone that have accumulated over millennia. Divers can observe firsthand the stratification of these layers, which tell a story of the reef's ancient past, including periods of rapid growth, erosion, and regrowth. Some caves also contain fossilized remains of marine organisms that lived millions of years ago, providing valuable insights into the historical biodiversity of the reef and the changes it has undergone through various environmental shifts.

The hidden caves of the Great Barrier Reef are not just of interest to recreational divers but also to marine biologists and geologists who study the unique ecosystems within these environments. The caves offer scientists a relatively undisturbed setting in which to observe and collect data on species that are difficult to study in other parts of the reef. By exploring these caves, researchers have been able to identify new species of marine life, some of which are entirely endemic to the cave systems and cannot be found anywhere else on Earth. These discoveries are crucial for understanding the overall biodiversity of the reef and for developing conservation strategies to protect these fragile ecosystems from human activities and environmental threats.

One of the key challenges to the preservation of the reef's cave systems is their vulnerability to environmental changes, particularly those brought on by climate change. Rising ocean temperatures, increased acidification, and pollution all pose significant threats to the delicate balance of life within the caves. Corals, which are already under stress from bleaching events in the more exposed parts of the reef, are also susceptible to these changes in the caves. While the deeper sections of the reef are somewhat insulated from immediate temperature fluctuations, prolonged environmental changes can still disrupt the delicate ecosystems within the caves, leading to a loss of biodiversity and the degradation of coral health.

In addition to climate change, human activities such as fishing, boating, and diving can also have a negative impact on the cave ecosystems. Although cave diving is a popular activity for experienced divers, improper diving practices can cause damage to the delicate coral formations and disturb the marine life that inhabits the caves. Accidental collisions with cave walls or careless handling of equipment can break corals and destroy habitats that have taken centuries to form. To mitigate these risks, many dive operators and marine parks in the Great Barrier Reef enforce strict guidelines for cave diving, ensuring that divers follow responsible practices and minimize their impact on the environment.

Protecting the hidden caves of the Great Barrier Reef is an important aspect of broader conservation efforts aimed at preserving the entire reef system. The caves are not just isolated pockets of biodiversity but are interconnected with the rest of the reef's ecosystems. The species that rely on the caves for shelter and breeding are often key players in the broader food webs of the reef, and any disruption to the cave ecosystems can have ripple effects throughout the reef. Conservation efforts that focus on reducing the impacts of climate change, pollution, and overfishing are essential for ensuring the long-term health of the reef's caves and the species that call them home.

For divers, scientists, and conservationists alike, the hidden caves of the Great Barrier Reef represent a fascinating and vital part of one of the world's most extraordinary natural wonders. Exploring these caves offers a rare glimpse into a world that few have the opportunity to witness, revealing the complex interplay between geology, marine biology, and environmental conservation. As more attention is focused on protecting the Great Barrier Reef from the myriad threats it faces, the hidden caves will continue to be a source of discovery, wonder, and hope for future generations seeking to understand and preserve this fragile ecosystem.

Chapter 16: The Importance of Seagrass Meadows in the Reef

Seagrass meadows, often overshadowed by the dazzling beauty of coral reefs, are one of the most crucial ecosystems within the Great Barrier Reef. These sprawling underwater grasslands are not just important for the health of the reef but also for the survival of countless marine species. Found in the shallow waters along the coastlines and lagoons of the Great Barrier Reef, seagrass meadows play an integral role in supporting the biodiversity, productivity, and resilience of this vast coral system. Despite their simple appearance, seagrass beds are vibrant ecosystems brimming with life and essential for the overall functioning of marine environments. They serve as nurseries, feeding grounds, and shelters for a wide range of species, from small fish to massive dugongs. Understanding the importance of seagrass meadows in the Great Barrier Reef reveals just how interconnected ocean ecosystems are, and highlights why these often-overlooked habitats must be protected alongside coral reefs.

Seagrass meadows are composed of flowering plants that grow in shallow, coastal waters where sunlight can penetrate to the seabed, allowing the plants to photosynthesize. Unlike seaweed, seagrasses are true plants, with roots, stems, and leaves. Their roots anchor them to the seabed, while their leaves form dense, grass-like structures that can spread across vast areas, creating a lush underwater landscape. These plants are highly efficient at capturing sunlight and nutrients, making them one of the most productive ecosystems on the planet. Seagrass meadows can be found in coastal regions all over the world, but those in the Great Barrier Reef are particularly significant due to their scale and biodiversity.

One of the most important roles seagrass meadows play in the Great Barrier Reef is as a nursery for juvenile marine life. The dense leaves of the seagrass provide a safe haven for young fish, crabs, shrimp, and other small organisms that need shelter from predators. The structure of the seagrass bed makes it difficult for larger predatory fish to navigate, offering these young creatures a refuge where they can grow and develop before moving out into the open waters of the reef. Species such as snapper, grouper, and emperor fish, which are vital to the reef's food web, often spend the early stages of their lives in seagrass meadows. By providing this essential nursery habitat, seagrass beds ensure the continued survival and replenishment of key species that are integral to the reef's ecosystem.

Seagrass meadows are also critical feeding grounds for several iconic species of the Great Barrier Reef. Perhaps the most famous of these is the dugong, a large marine mammal closely related to the manatee. Dugongs, often referred to as "sea cows," graze almost exclusively on seagrass, spending their days feeding in the meadows and maintaining the health of these ecosystems through their grazing behavior. Dugongs play a vital role in controlling the growth of seagrass, ensuring that the meadows remain healthy and productive. By feeding on older, less nutritious seagrass, dugongs allow new, more nutrient-rich seagrass to grow, which benefits the entire ecosystem. Without the presence of dugongs, seagrass meadows could become overgrown and less effective at supporting marine life.

In addition to dugongs, green sea turtles are another species that rely heavily on seagrass meadows for their survival. Green sea turtles are herbivores and graze on the seagrass as a primary food source. Like dugongs, their grazing helps to keep the seagrass meadows healthy and prevents overgrowth. The health of the green sea turtle population is directly tied to the health of the seagrass meadows, making these habitats essential for the continued survival of this endangered species. Turtles, in turn, play a significant role in the reef ecosystem by maintaining the balance of seagrass growth, preventing the meadows from becoming too dense and promoting biodiversity.

Seagrass meadows are not only important for the animals that graze on them, but they also serve as a habitat for a wide range of other species. The thick seagrass provides shelter for many invertebrates, including sea cucumbers, sea urchins, and various types of mollusks. These invertebrates form an essential part of the food chain, supporting higher trophic levels such as fish, birds, and marine mammals. Seagrass beds are also home to a variety of crustaceans, such as crabs and shrimp, which contribute to the overall productivity of the ecosystem. The diversity of species that inhabit seagrass meadows makes them one of the most ecologically important habitats in the reef.

Beyond their biological importance, seagrass meadows play a critical role in the physical environment of the reef. They act as natural filters, trapping sediments and pollutants that would otherwise flow into the coral reef and damage the delicate coral polyps. By stabilizing the seabed with their root systems, seagrass beds prevent erosion and reduce the amount of sediment that gets stirred up by ocean currents or human activities. This filtering action is vital for maintaining the clarity and quality of the water in the reef, which is essential for the health of coral and other marine organisms. Seagrass meadows also act as carbon sinks, capturing and storing large amounts of carbon dioxide from the atmosphere. This makes them an important tool in the fight against climate change, as they help to mitigate the effects of increasing carbon emissions by sequestering carbon in their biomass and in the sediments beneath them.

Despite their importance, seagrass meadows are facing numerous threats that put their survival at risk. Human activities such as coastal development, dredging, and pollution have caused significant damage to seagrass habitats in many parts of the world, including the Great Barrier Reef. When sediments from construction or dredging projects are released into the water, they can smother seagrass beds, blocking sunlight and inhibiting their ability to photosynthesize. Pollution from agricultural runoff, sewage, and industrial waste also poses a significant threat to seagrass meadows, introducing harmful chemicals and nutrients into the water that can lead to algal blooms. These blooms can outcompete seagrass for sunlight and oxygen, leading to the decline of the meadow and the loss of the species that depend on it.

Another major threat to seagrass meadows is climate change. Rising ocean temperatures can cause heat stress to seagrass, inhibiting their growth and reducing their resilience to other environmental pressures. Additionally, ocean acidification, caused by the increasing absorption of carbon dioxide by the ocean, can weaken the structure of seagrass plants and make it harder for them to reproduce. Sea level rise, another consequence of climate change, can also threaten seagrass meadows by altering the shallow coastal environments where they thrive. As sea levels rise, seagrass beds may be forced to migrate to shallower waters, but in many cases, human development along coastlines prevents this natural migration, leading to the loss of valuable habitat.

To protect seagrass meadows and ensure their continued role in the health of the Great Barrier Reef, conservation efforts must focus on reducing the impact of human activities and mitigating the effects of climate change. Establishing marine protected areas that include seagrass meadows is one of the most effective ways to safeguard these ecosystems. In these protected areas, activities such as dredging, fishing, and boating are restricted or regulated to minimize damage to seagrass habitats. Restoration efforts, such as replanting damaged seagrass beds, are also being used in some areas to help revive these ecosystems. However, preventing further damage is key, as seagrass meadows can take decades to recover once they have been destroyed.

Public awareness and education are also crucial for the protection of seagrass meadows. Many people are unaware of the important role seagrass plays in the health of the Great Barrier Reef and the broader marine environment. By educating communities, especially those living near coastal areas, about the importance of seagrass and the threats it faces, individuals can be encouraged to take actions that reduce their impact on these ecosystems. Simple steps such as reducing pollution, supporting sustainable fishing practices, and participating in conservation programs can make a significant difference in the protection of seagrass meadows.

Seagrass meadows are an often-overlooked but vital component of the Great Barrier Reef's ecosystem. Their importance extends beyond their role as a habitat for marine life, as they also contribute to the physical health of the reef, support biodiversity, and combat climate change. Protecting these valuable habitats is essential for the long-term health of the Great Barrier Reef and the many species that depend on it. As we continue to explore and understand the intricate connections between different marine ecosystems, it becomes clear that the survival of seagrass meadows is inextricably linked to the survival of the reef itself.

Chapter 17: Unique Species Found Only in the Reef

The Great Barrier Reef is renowned for being one of the most biodiverse ecosystems on Earth, and it hosts an astonishing array of unique species that cannot be found anywhere else. This vast coral system stretches over 2,300 kilometers along the northeastern coast of Australia, providing the ideal habitat for a wide range of marine life. Its unique combination of warm, shallow waters, complex coral structures, and abundant seagrass meadows has allowed for the evolution and preservation of countless species, many of which are endemic to the reef. The presence of such distinctive creatures highlights the reef's irreplaceable value to both science and the natural world, as it serves as a living laboratory where species evolve in response to specific environmental conditions.

One of the most iconic and unique species of the Great Barrier Reef is the reef's own green turtle population. Although green turtles are found in oceans around the world, the population that nests on the islands and beaches of the Great Barrier Reef is genetically distinct from others. These turtles are an essential part of the reef ecosystem, playing a crucial role in maintaining the health of seagrass meadows by grazing on the grass, preventing overgrowth, and ensuring that the ecosystem remains balanced. However, these turtles are particularly vulnerable to the threats posed by climate change, habitat destruction, and pollution. Because the Great Barrier Reef is home to one of the largest green turtle nesting sites globally, the protection of this species is closely tied to the health of the reef itself.

The reef is also home to an astonishing variety of fish species, many of which are found nowhere else. One of the most notable is the brightly colored Parrotfish, a key player in the health of coral ecosystems. There are several species of Parrotfish endemic to the Great

Barrier Reef, such as the Yellowbarred Parrotfish. These fish have a specialized diet that consists largely of algae, which they scrape off coral with their strong, beak-like teeth. In doing so, Parrotfish help prevent algae from overgrowing and suffocating coral, ensuring that the reef remains vibrant and healthy. Their feeding habits also play a unique role in coral reef dynamics, as they ingest pieces of coral rock, grind it down, and excrete it as sand, which contributes to the sandy beaches found in the region.

The reef is home to numerous species of damselfish, some of which are endemic to this ecosystem. The Lemon Damselfish, distinguished by its striking yellow coloration, can only be found in the waters of the Great Barrier Reef. This small but territorial fish plays a role in the health of coral, as it often resides in close association with certain types of coral, using them as protection against predators and, in turn, helping to keep coral-eating species in check. The damselfish's complex social behaviors and relationships with their coral habitats highlight the delicate balance between species that exists within the reef system.

Beyond fish, the Great Barrier Reef is home to numerous species of mollusks, many of which are exclusive to this region. One of the most extraordinary examples is the Fluted Giant Clam (Tridacna squamosa), a species of enormous, brightly colored clam that is only found within the boundaries of the reef. These clams, which can grow up to 1.2 meters in length, are important reef inhabitants. They host symbiotic algae within their tissues, which helps them produce energy from sunlight through photosynthesis, similar to how coral relies on zooxanthellae. The Giant Clam's vibrant, iridescent colors come from these algae, which live in harmony with the clam. Their presence on the reef is a testament to the intricate and interconnected relationships that thrive within this ecosystem, as clams provide shelter for smaller creatures while contributing to the reef's productivity.

The Great Barrier Reef is also famous for its rare and unique species of sea stars, including the Crown-of-Thorns Starfish (Acanthaster planci). While not exclusive to the reef, this species has a particular prominence here due to its potential to become a destructive force if left unchecked. The Crown-of-Thorns Starfish feeds on coral polyps, and when its population surges, it can cause widespread damage to coral reefs. This starfish's complex role in the reef ecosystem highlights the delicate balance between species, as the unchecked growth of the Crown-of-Thorns population can lead to coral degradation, affecting the broader biodiversity of the region. Efforts to manage the population of this starfish through manual removal and other conservation efforts underscore the importance of understanding and maintaining species balance in the reef.

Another group of species unique to the Great Barrier Reef includes its vast array of soft corals and sea fans. While hard corals often get most of the attention due to their role in forming the physical structure of the reef, soft corals are equally important and often overlooked. Soft corals, such as those belonging to the family Alcyoniidae, create vast fields of vibrant, colorful colonies in the deeper and more sheltered areas of the reef. These corals provide critical habitat for many species of fish and invertebrates, offering both shelter and food. The diversity of soft corals found in the Great Barrier Reef is unparalleled, with some species being entirely endemic to the region due to its unique environmental conditions.

The reef is also home to various species of sea snakes, some of which are endemic to this part of the world. The Olive Sea Snake, for instance, is one of the most common and is uniquely adapted to life in the warm, shallow waters of the reef. This species, along with others, plays a role as both predator and prey, maintaining the balance of species within the reef. Sea snakes are excellent swimmers, and their streamlined bodies allow them to navigate through the intricate coral formations. Despite their venomous nature, sea snakes are generally not aggressive towards humans and play an important role in controlling populations of small fish and other prey species.

The Great Barrier Reef is also known for its unique and colorful nudibranchs, a type of sea slug that is especially abundant in the region. Nudibranchs, often referred to as "sea butterflies," are celebrated for their vivid and striking colors, which make them a popular sight for divers and marine biologists alike. Some species of nudibranch are endemic to the reef, having evolved specialized diets and behaviors that are perfectly suited to the unique coral and sponge environments found here. These tiny but vibrant creatures are a testament to the remarkable biodiversity of the reef and its ability to support even the most specialized forms of life.

One of the most elusive and fascinating creatures found in the Great Barrier Reef is the pygmy seahorse. These tiny seahorses, which measure less than two centimeters in length, are masters of camouflage and can only be found in specific coral habitats within the reef. They are so well camouflaged that they are almost indistinguishable from the coral they live on, making them incredibly difficult to spot even by experienced divers. The pygmy seahorse's ability to blend in with its environment is an example of the highly specialized adaptations that many reef species have developed to survive in this complex ecosystem. These creatures are rarely seen outside the reef, making them a true marvel of the biodiversity found in this underwater wonderland.

The Great Barrier Reef's invertebrate population is equally as unique as its fish and coral inhabitants. The Peacock Mantis Shrimp, for example, is a strikingly colorful and aggressive predator found in the reef's rocky crevices. Known for its powerful punch, which can break the shells of its prey and even crack aquarium glass, this shrimp is one of the most formidable hunters in the reef. It possesses one of the most complex visual systems in the animal kingdom, capable of seeing polarized light and a broad spectrum of colors. The Peacock Mantis Shrimp's presence in the Great Barrier Reef exemplifies the reef's role as a hotspot for extraordinary and highly specialized species that push the boundaries of biological diversity.

Other unique species that are synonymous with the Great Barrier Reef include various species of sponges, jellyfish, and sea anemones. One particularly interesting species is the Irukandji jellyfish, a small but incredibly venomous jellyfish that is found primarily in the northern parts of the reef. Despite its diminutive size, the Irukandji jellyfish has a powerful sting that can cause severe pain and even life-threatening symptoms in humans. These jellyfish are a reminder of the reef's natural challenges and the need for caution when exploring such a complex and diverse environment. The diversity of jellyfish species in the Great Barrier Reef also points to the varied niches that exist within the ecosystem, where even the most specialized species can find a home.

In summary, the Great Barrier Reef is not only the largest coral system in the world but also a unique repository of species found nowhere else on Earth. From genetically distinct populations of turtles to vibrant fish, rare invertebrates, and elusive sea creatures, the reef's biodiversity is a testament to millions of years of evolution and adaptation. Each species, whether it plays a visible or hidden role in the ecosystem, contributes to the reef's intricate and interconnected web of life. This vast array of endemic species highlights the importance of protecting the reef from the various threats it faces, including climate change, pollution, and overfishing, as losing any of these unique species would mean losing a vital part of this extraordinary natural wonder.

Chapter 18: How Scientists Study and Monitor the Reef

Studying and monitoring the Great Barrier Reef is an incredibly complex, multifaceted task that requires collaboration between marine biologists, oceanographers, climate scientists, and ecologists, among others. Given its immense size, the reef spans over 344,000 square kilometers and consists of nearly 3,000 individual reefs. As the largest coral system in the world, it plays a critical role in marine ecosystems and biodiversity, so ensuring its health is a global priority. Scientists employ a wide range of methods, from cutting-edge technology to traditional fieldwork, to understand the reef's condition, assess the impact of human activities and environmental changes, and formulate strategies for conservation.

One of the fundamental ways scientists study the Great Barrier Reef is through field surveys. These on-the-ground surveys involve marine biologists and divers who travel to different sections of the reef to collect data firsthand. This involves identifying species, documenting coral health, measuring water quality, and observing changes in the reef structure. Divers might swim along set transects—measured sections of the reef—collecting data on the abundance and variety of coral and fish species, the presence of diseases, and the degree of coral bleaching. These surveys provide direct insight into how different areas of the reef are faring and help scientists detect localized issues, such as overfishing, pollution, or physical damage caused by human activities like tourism and boating.

One key aspect of field surveys is the monitoring of coral health, which includes assessing the levels of coral bleaching. Coral bleaching occurs when corals, stressed by environmental factors like warming ocean temperatures, expel the symbiotic algae living within their tissues. These algae, known as zooxanthellae, provide the coral with much of its energy and its vibrant colors. Without these algae, corals turn white and become more susceptible to disease and death. Scientists monitor coral bleaching using a variety of methods, including visual assessments by divers and the use of drones or satellites to detect large-scale bleaching events. Visual assessments allow scientists to examine individual corals for signs of bleaching, such as changes in color or tissue loss, while aerial or satellite imagery can reveal bleaching across vast swaths of the reef.

In addition to field surveys, scientists rely on advanced technology to monitor the reef more comprehensively. One of the most critical tools is remote sensing, which uses satellites and drones equipped with specialized cameras and sensors to capture detailed images of the reef from above. These high-resolution images allow scientists to map the structure of the reef, observe changes in coral cover, and track the health of the reef over time. Remote sensing is particularly valuable because it provides a bird's-eye view of the reef, enabling scientists to detect patterns that may not be visible from underwater surveys. For instance, satellites can monitor changes in sea surface temperature, which is a significant factor in coral bleaching, and detect shifts in the color of the reef, indicating large-scale bleaching or algal overgrowth.

Another technological advancement used in reef monitoring is underwater robotics. Autonomous underwater vehicles (AUVs) and remotely operated vehicles (ROVs) are deployed to explore deeper parts of the reef that are difficult for human divers to access. These underwater robots are equipped with cameras, sonar, and other sensors that can capture detailed images and data from the depths of the reef. AUVs and ROVs can travel to areas beyond the reach of traditional scuba diving, allowing scientists to study deep-water corals and ecosystems that are less understood but equally important to the reef's overall health. These robots can also operate in conditions that would be dangerous or impractical for human divers, such as during storms or at extreme depths, making them invaluable tools for continuous monitoring.

Coral reef monitoring also involves the use of underwater monitoring stations, which are permanent or semi-permanent installations placed in various locations across the reef. These stations are equipped with instruments that continuously measure a range of environmental parameters, such as water temperature, pH levels, salinity, and nutrient concentrations. This real-time data collection allows scientists to detect changes in the reef's environment quickly, providing an early warning system for potential threats. For example, if water temperatures rise suddenly, scientists can anticipate an increased risk of coral bleaching and take steps to mitigate the impact, such as implementing temporary fishing bans or limiting tourism in vulnerable areas.

Water quality monitoring is another critical component of reef research, as the health of the Great Barrier Reef is heavily influenced by the quality of the surrounding waters. Runoff from agriculture, industrial activities, and urban development can introduce pollutants like pesticides, fertilizers, and sediments into the ocean, which can harm coral and marine life. Scientists monitor water quality by collecting water samples from various locations across the reef and analyzing them for the presence of harmful substances. This monitoring helps identify the sources of pollution and track how these pollutants are affecting different areas of the reef. In addition to collecting water samples, researchers also use sensors attached to buoys or underwater stations to measure water quality parameters continuously. These sensors provide valuable data on changes in water chemistry, which can be used to assess the impact of pollution on the reef ecosystem over time.

Ocean acidification, driven by the increased absorption of carbon dioxide (CO_2) by the oceans, is another major threat to coral reefs that scientists are actively studying. As CO_2 levels in the atmosphere rise, more of the gas dissolves in seawater, forming carbonic acid. This acid lowers the pH of the water, making it more difficult for corals to build their calcium carbonate skeletons. To monitor the effects of ocean acidification on the Great Barrier Reef, scientists measure the pH levels of the water and study how changes in acidity are affecting coral growth and reef structure. This research is critical for understanding how the reef might respond to future changes in the climate and for developing strategies to mitigate the impacts of acidification.

In addition to studying the physical and chemical aspects of the reef, scientists are also focused on understanding the behavior and biology of the species that inhabit the reef. This includes tracking the movements and population dynamics of key species, such as fish, turtles, and sharks. One method used to study marine species is tagging, where scientists attach small tracking devices to animals to monitor their movements over time. These tags can provide valuable data on the migration patterns, feeding habits, and reproductive behaviors of species that are critical to the health of the reef ecosystem. For example, tracking the movements of sharks can help scientists understand their role as top predators in maintaining the balance of the reef's food web.

Genetic research is also playing an increasingly important role in reef monitoring and conservation. Scientists are using genetic techniques to study the diversity and health of coral populations, as well as to identify species that may be more resilient to environmental stressors like rising temperatures or pollution. By analyzing the genetic makeup of corals, researchers can identify individuals or populations with traits that make them more resistant to bleaching or disease. This information can then be used to inform conservation strategies, such as selectively breeding corals with these resilient traits in restoration efforts or protecting areas where these resilient populations are found.

Citizen science initiatives have become a valuable part of the effort to study and monitor the Great Barrier Reef. Programs like the Great

Barrier Reef Marine Park Authority's (GBRMPA) "Eye on the Reef" allow tourists, local residents, and recreational divers to contribute to the scientific understanding of the reef by submitting observations and photos of coral, fish, and other marine life. These citizen scientists help gather data from a wider range of locations than would be possible with professional researchers alone, providing a more comprehensive picture of the reef's condition. The data collected through these initiatives is used to track changes in the reef's biodiversity and health over time, and to identify emerging threats that may require further investigation.

Long-term monitoring programs are essential for understanding the changes occurring in the Great Barrier Reef over time. One of the most prominent programs is the Australian Institute of Marine Science's (AIMS) Long-Term Monitoring Program (LTMP), which has been collecting data on the reef's health since 1985. The LTMP focuses on tracking coral cover, fish populations, and the presence of species like the Crown-of-Thorns starfish, a coral predator that can cause significant damage to the reef if its population becomes too large. The data from the LTMP is invaluable for detecting long-term trends in the reef's health and for understanding how the reef is responding to threats like climate change, overfishing, and pollution.

Another critical area of research is the development of coral restoration techniques. Scientists are exploring methods for helping coral reefs recover from damage caused by bleaching, storms, or human activities. One promising technique is coral gardening, where small fragments of healthy coral are grown in underwater nurseries and then transplanted to damaged areas of the reef. This method has shown success in helping to restore coral cover in some parts of the Great Barrier Reef. Researchers are also experimenting with assisted evolution, a technique that involves selectively breeding corals with traits that make them more resilient to stressors like warming temperatures or acidification. By fostering the growth of more resilient coral species, scientists hope to give the reef a better chance of surviving the challenges posed by climate change.

In conclusion, the study and monitoring of the Great Barrier Reef involve a vast array of techniques and technologies, each contributing to a better understanding of this complex and vital ecosystem. From field surveys and remote sensing to genetic research and citizen science, the combined efforts of scientists around the world are helping to safeguard the future of the reef. As the reef faces increasing threats from climate change, pollution, and human activity, the work of these researchers is more important than ever in ensuring that the Great Barrier Reef continues to thrive for generations to come.

Chapter 19: The Role of the Reef in Coastal Communities

The Great Barrier Reef plays a vital and multifaceted role in supporting coastal communities, particularly those in northeastern Australia where the reef is located. Its importance extends beyond the dazzling marine ecosystem it sustains; it provides substantial economic, social, and cultural benefits to millions of people. For the coastal communities that depend on the reef, it is an indispensable natural asset that influences their way of life, livelihoods, and cultural identity. Understanding the various ways the reef contributes to these communities can provide insight into why protecting the reef is a global priority.

One of the most direct ways the Great Barrier Reef supports coastal communities is through its contribution to the local and national economy, especially in terms of tourism. As one of the most iconic natural wonders of the world, the reef draws millions of visitors each year who come to experience its stunning biodiversity, clear blue waters, and vibrant coral formations. The tourism industry surrounding the reef is vast, encompassing activities like snorkeling, diving, boating, reef cruises, and eco-tours. This influx of tourists generates significant revenue for local businesses, including hotels, restaurants, tour operators, and shops. According to various estimates, the reef-related tourism industry contributes billions of dollars to Australia's economy annually, making it one of the most lucrative natural tourism destinations in the world.

The benefits of tourism ripple through coastal communities by creating employment opportunities. Thousands of people are employed directly in tourism-related jobs, such as dive instructors, boat captains, guides, hospitality workers, and marine conservation specialists. Indirectly, the tourism industry also supports jobs in sectors like transportation, retail, and manufacturing, as businesses that cater to tourists rely on local suppliers and infrastructure. For many coastal towns along the northeastern coast of Australia, tourism associated with the reef is the backbone of their economies. Without the steady stream of visitors drawn to the reef's beauty and marine biodiversity, many of these communities would face significant economic challenges.

Apart from tourism, the Great Barrier Reef is also essential for commercial and recreational fishing, another crucial industry for coastal communities. The reef's rich biodiversity supports a wide variety of fish species that are integral to the livelihoods of fishers and the local seafood industry. Commercial fisheries rely on the reef's ecosystem to provide a steady supply of fish, crustaceans, and mollusks that are harvested and sold both domestically and internationally. Species such as coral trout, red emperor, prawns, and lobsters are particularly valuable and form the basis of many fishing operations in the region.

The sustainability of commercial fishing in the reef region is closely tied to the health of the reef's ecosystem. The coral structures, seagrass meadows, and mangrove forests provide critical habitats for fish species at various stages of their life cycles, from breeding and spawning to feeding and sheltering. Maintaining the health of these habitats is essential for ensuring the long-term productivity of fisheries. This, in turn, means that the health of the reef has a direct impact on the economic well-being of fishing communities. Overfishing, pollution, and climate change can threaten these delicate ecosystems, which is why sustainable fishing practices and reef conservation efforts are so important for preserving both marine biodiversity and the livelihoods of fishers.

In addition to commercial fishing, the reef also supports recreational fishing, which is a popular activity among locals and tourists alike. Recreational fishing contributes to the economy through the purchase of equipment, boat rentals, fuel, and other related services. Moreover, recreational fishing has deep cultural and social significance for many coastal communities, as it provides an opportunity for people to connect with nature, engage in traditional practices, and pass on fishing knowledge to younger generations. For Indigenous communities, fishing in the reef's waters holds even greater importance, as it is tied to cultural traditions and ancestral rights. Many Indigenous groups have fished these waters for thousands of years, relying on the reef's resources for food and sustenance while also developing deep spiritual and cultural ties to the land and sea.

The cultural significance of the Great Barrier Reef to Indigenous communities cannot be overstated. For thousands of years, Indigenous Australians have lived in harmony with the reef, using its resources for food, shelter, tools, and spiritual practices. The reef is deeply intertwined with the stories, traditions, and customs of many Indigenous groups, and it holds a sacred place in their belief systems. These communities view the reef not just as a natural resource, but as an integral part of their cultural heritage. Indigenous knowledge of the reef, passed down through generations, includes a profound understanding of the rhythms of the ocean, the behavior of marine species, and the importance of sustainability. Many Indigenous groups continue to practice traditional hunting and fishing techniques that are in balance with the reef's ecosystem, ensuring that they take only what they need and leave the environment healthy for future generations.

In recent years, Indigenous communities have played an increasingly active role in the management and conservation of the Great Barrier Reef. Co-management agreements between the Australian government and Indigenous groups have recognized the importance of traditional ecological knowledge in maintaining the health of the reef. Indigenous rangers work alongside scientists and conservationists to monitor the reef, manage marine protected areas, and implement strategies to reduce human impact on the ecosystem.

This collaboration between modern science and traditional practices has been instrumental in improving the conservation and sustainable use of the reef's resources.

Beyond economic and cultural contributions, the Great Barrier Reef also provides critical environmental services that benefit coastal communities, one of the most important being coastal protection. Coral reefs act as natural barriers, absorbing the energy of waves and storm surges before they reach the shore. This buffering effect helps to protect coastal areas from erosion, flooding, and damage caused by tropical storms and cyclones. For communities that are vulnerable to extreme weather events, the reef's role in coastal defense is invaluable. Without the protective barrier provided by the reef, many coastal towns and cities would be far more susceptible to the impacts of rising sea levels and increasingly powerful storms driven by climate change.

The reef's capacity to protect coastal infrastructure, homes, and natural habitats from storm damage has enormous economic and social implications. In areas where coral reefs have been degraded or lost due to coral bleaching, pollution, or human activity, coastal communities face a higher risk of experiencing severe damage during extreme weather events. The cost of rebuilding and repairing infrastructure, as well as the disruption to livelihoods, can be devastating. As such, preserving the health of the reef is not only essential for maintaining marine biodiversity but also for safeguarding the safety and well-being of coastal populations.

The Great Barrier Reef also contributes to the health and stability of marine ecosystems beyond its immediate borders. Its role in nutrient cycling and as a habitat for a vast array of species helps to maintain the balance of marine life in the surrounding waters. The interconnectedness of marine ecosystems means that the health of the reef has far-reaching effects on the broader ocean environment. Healthy coral reefs support seagrass meadows, mangroves, and other coastal ecosystems, which in turn provide essential services such as carbon sequestration, water filtration, and habitat for a wide range of marine species.

Seagrass meadows, which are found in and around the Great Barrier Reef, play a crucial role in supporting coastal communities by acting as nurseries for many fish species that are vital to both commercial and subsistence fishing. These underwater grasslands also help to stabilize sediment, reduce coastal erosion, and improve water quality by filtering pollutants. The health of seagrass meadows is closely linked to the health of the reef, as both ecosystems rely on clear, nutrient-rich waters to thrive. When coral reefs are damaged or degraded, it can have a cascading effect on the surrounding ecosystems, including seagrass meadows, which further underscores the importance of protecting the reef for the benefit of coastal communities.

In conclusion, the Great Barrier Reef is an irreplaceable natural asset that supports coastal communities in a multitude of ways. From driving tourism and providing livelihoods through fishing to protecting coastlines from storms and fostering cultural connections, the reef's contributions are essential to the well-being of millions of people. The economic, social, and environmental benefits it provides are deeply interconnected, and any threat to the reef's health has direct consequences for the communities that depend on it. As the reef faces increasing pressures from climate change, pollution, and human activity, the need to protect and preserve it for future generations becomes ever more urgent. Coastal communities, both Indigenous and non-Indigenous, have a critical role to play in the stewardship of the reef, and their continued involvement in conservation efforts is key to ensuring the long-term survival of this natural wonder. By understanding and valuing the reef's role in supporting these communities, we can better appreciate the importance of maintaining its health and integrity for the future.

Chapter 20: Amazing Reef Symbiosis: Partnerships in Nature

The Great Barrier Reef is one of the most biologically diverse ecosystems on Earth, and at its core lies a delicate web of relationships between its many inhabitants. The term "symbiosis" refers to the interaction between two different organisms living in close physical proximity, often to the benefit of one or both. In the vibrant underwater world of the reef, symbiosis is not just common; it's essential to the survival of many species and the overall health of the ecosystem. The interconnectedness of life on the reef showcases nature's incredible capacity for cooperation, adaptation, and balance.

One of the most well-known and fascinating examples of symbiosis in the Great Barrier Reef is the relationship between coral and zooxanthellae, tiny single-celled algae that live inside coral tissues. This relationship is a classic example of mutualism, a type of symbiosis where both organisms benefit. Coral reefs are made up of millions of tiny coral polyps, each of which secretes a calcium carbonate skeleton that forms the structure of the reef. However, corals need more than just their skeletons to thrive in the nutrient-poor waters of the tropics. That's where zooxanthellae come in.

The algae live within the coral's tissues, where they use sunlight to perform photosynthesis, converting carbon dioxide and water into sugars and oxygen. These sugars provide the coral with most of its energy, fueling its growth and helping it build its reef structures. In return, the coral provides the zooxanthellae with a protected environment and the compounds necessary for photosynthesis. This relationship is so crucial that the survival of coral reefs depends on it. When corals become stressed due to rising water temperatures or other environmental changes, they can expel the zooxanthellae, leading to a condition known as coral bleaching. Without the energy provided by the algae, the corals turn white and can die if the symbiotic relationship is not restored.

This algae-coral partnership is just one of many examples of symbiosis that make the Great Barrier Reef such a thriving and complex environment. Another fascinating example is the relationship between certain species of fish and cleaner shrimp. Cleaner shrimp and cleaner fish, such as the cleaner wrasse, provide a much-needed service to other marine animals by removing parasites, dead skin, and debris from their scales and skin. This interaction is also mutualistic because both the cleaner and the client species benefit. The cleaner gets a meal, while the client fish or animal gets rid of harmful parasites that could weaken or kill them. This cleaning behavior often takes place at "cleaning stations," where fish, eels, and even large creatures like sea turtles and sharks line up to be serviced by the cleaners.

What makes this relationship even more fascinating is the level of trust between the cleaner and the client. Often, the cleaner is much smaller than the client, yet the larger animal refrains from eating the cleaner, knowing that the service provided is worth the restraint. In some cases, cleaner shrimp will even enter the mouths of larger fish to clean out parasites from their gills and teeth. This display of trust is one of the most remarkable aspects of symbiosis on the reef and underscores the intricate balance that exists between different species.

Another intriguing symbiotic relationship found in the Great Barrier Reef is between clownfish and sea anemones. Clownfish, made famous by movies like *Finding Nemo*, live among the venomous tentacles of sea anemones, which would sting and kill most other fish. However, clownfish have a special mucus coating on their skin that protects them from the anemone's stings. In return for the protection that the anemone provides, the clownfish help keep the anemone clean by removing debris and parasites. The clownfish also bring food to the anemone in the form of small prey they catch. This mutually beneficial relationship allows both species to thrive, with the clownfish finding a safe home and the anemone benefiting from extra nourishment.

The symbiosis between certain types of crabs and corals is another fascinating example of how cooperation helps maintain balance in the reef ecosystem. Some species of crabs, such as the Trapezia crab, live among the branches of corals. These crabs defend their coral hosts from predators like crown-of-thorns starfish, which can devastate coral populations. In exchange for this protection, the crabs are provided with a safe habitat and food in the form of mucus produced by the coral. The relationship helps ensure that coral colonies can grow and thrive, while the crabs have a stable and secure home.

Symbiosis in the Great Barrier Reef isn't limited to just two species. Often, entire groups of organisms are involved in complex interactions that benefit multiple members of the ecosystem. One example is the relationship between parrotfish, coral reefs, and seagrass meadows. Parrotfish play an essential role in maintaining the health of coral reefs by grazing on algae that can otherwise overgrow and smother corals. By keeping algal populations in check, parrotfish allow corals to flourish. In turn, healthy coral reefs provide habitat for a variety of marine species, including those that rely on seagrass meadows for food and shelter.

Seagrass meadows themselves are another critical component of the reef ecosystem, and they too depend on symbiotic relationships for their survival. Dugongs, large marine mammals closely related to manatees, are one of the primary grazers of seagrass. By feeding on seagrass, dugongs help keep these underwater meadows healthy by preventing overgrowth and promoting new seagrass shoots. This grazing activity allows seagrass meadows to continue providing habitat for juvenile fish, turtles, and other marine species. Seagrass meadows also help protect the coastline from erosion, making them a vital part of the coastal ecosystem.

Another remarkable form of symbiosis in the Great Barrier Reef involves sea sponges and various species of reef-dwelling fish. Sea sponges are filter feeders that help maintain water quality by filtering out bacteria, plankton, and organic particles from the water. In return, some species of fish use sponges as shelter, hiding among their structures to avoid predators. The sponges benefit from the fish's presence because the fish help clean the sponges by removing debris and deterring parasites. This relationship improves the overall health of the reef's waters and provides a safe haven for smaller fish species.

One cannot discuss symbiosis on the Great Barrier Reef without mentioning the intricate relationship between mangroves, coral reefs, and the creatures that depend on both ecosystems. Mangroves grow in the shallow coastal waters adjacent to the reef, and their complex root systems provide a critical nursery habitat for many marine species, including fish, crabs, and shrimp. The roots of mangroves trap sediments and nutrients, preventing them from flowing onto the coral reef and smothering it. In return, the coral reef helps protect the mangroves from strong wave action, creating a symbiotic relationship between these two vital ecosystems. This connection ensures that both habitats can support a wide range of species, from juvenile fish in the mangroves to the larger predators and herbivores on the reef.

Symbiosis is also seen in the interactions between various species of marine invertebrates, such as sea cucumbers and reef sediments. Sea cucumbers play a critical role in the reef ecosystem by feeding on detritus and organic matter found in the sediment. As they feed, they process and recycle nutrients, which helps keep the reef's sediment healthy and rich in nutrients. In turn, the health of the sediment supports the growth of seagrass and coral, which are vital to the overall structure of the reef. This type of nutrient cycling is an essential aspect of the reef's ecosystem, and it showcases how even the smallest organisms play a vital role in maintaining the health of the environment.

In addition to mutualistic relationships, the Great Barrier Reef is also home to other types of symbiosis, such as commensalism and parasitism. In commensalism, one species benefits from the relationship while the other is neither helped nor harmed. An example of this is the relationship between certain species of small fish and large marine animals like sea turtles or sharks. These small fish, often referred to as "hitchhikers," attach themselves to the bodies of larger animals to catch a free ride through the water. While the fish benefit from the mobility and protection offered by their larger host, the host animal is generally unaffected by the presence of the hitchhiker.

Parasitism, on the other hand, is a type of symbiosis where one organism benefits at the expense of the other. While parasitism is not as common in the reef as mutualism or commensalism, it still plays a role in the ecosystem. For example, some species of marine worms and crustaceans act as parasites, attaching themselves to the skin or gills of fish and feeding on their blood or tissues. While these parasites can harm individual fish, they also help maintain the balance of the ecosystem by controlling populations and preventing overpopulation of certain species.

In conclusion, the Great Barrier Reef is a living testament to the power of symbiosis in nature. The partnerships formed between its many inhabitants create a network of relationships that support the health, diversity, and resilience of the ecosystem. Whether it's the mutualistic bond between coral and algae, the cleaning services provided by shrimp and wrasse, or the complex interplay between mangroves and coral reefs, symbiosis is the key to understanding how life on the reef thrives. Each organism, no matter how small or seemingly insignificant, plays a role in this intricate dance of cooperation, and it is this balance that ensures the survival of the reef's unique and vibrant community. As we continue to study and appreciate the wonders of the reef, it becomes clear that the preservation of these symbiotic relationships is crucial to protecting one of the world's most extraordinary ecosystems for future generations.

Epilogue

We've reached the end of our journey through the Great Barrier Reef, and what an adventure it's been! From the bright corals and playful fish to the mysterious shipwrecks and gentle sea turtles, we've explored a world filled with wonders. The Great Barrier Reef is more than just a beautiful place—it's a vital part of our planet, teeming with life and holding secrets that help us understand our oceans and ourselves.

As you close this book, I hope you take away a deep appreciation for the magic that lies beneath the waves. The reef is not only a home for countless creatures but also a reminder of how connected our world truly is. Every piece of coral, every fish, and even every grain of sand has a role to play in keeping this delicate ecosystem in balance.

But the story doesn't end here. The Great Barrier Reef needs us all to be its protectors. Whether by learning more about ocean conservation, spreading the word about its beauty, or making choices that help protect the environment, we can all play a part in keeping this amazing place healthy for years to come.

Thank you for joining me on this adventure. I hope you continue to explore, to learn, and to dream about the wonders of our natural world. The Great Barrier Reef will always be there, waiting beneath the waves, full of color, life, and possibility—an underwater treasure that belongs to us all.

The End.